ROADS ARE NOT ENOUGH

ROADS ARE NOT ENOUGH

New perspectives on rural transport planning in developing countries

JONATHAN DAWSON and IAN BARWELL

INTERMEDIATE TECHNOLOGY PUBLICATIONS 1993

Published by Intermediate Technology Publications
103/105 Southampton Row, London WC1B 4HH, UK

© Intermediate Technology Publications 1993

British Library Cataloguing in Publication Data
Dawson, Jonathan
Roads are Not Enough: New Perspectives on
Rural Transport Planning in Developing Countries
I. Title   II. Barwell, Ian
388.09173

ISBN 1-85339-191-3

Typeset by J&L Composition Ltd, Filey, North Yorkshire
Printed in Great Britain by SRP Exeter

Contents

Foreword

TRANSPORT IS OF particular importance in rural areas of developing countries, providing rural people with access to the range of goods and services that they require to meet their daily needs, and for economic and social development. Access to ideas and information, to markets and services, to people and places, and to new opportunities, are all of crucial importance in the development process. But transport policy and programmes are often too narrowly defined in terms of a public sector responsibility for the development of the physical infrastructure for transport, principally roads. The work presented here aims to increase understanding of the transport needs of rural people, and of the range of policy options and programme measures to provide rural people with the access that they require.

The International Labour Organisation (ILO) and the Intermediate Technology Development Group (ITDG) have long been concerned with understanding the real nature of the transport needs of rural people, and they have worked to develop and implement measures to respond to those needs. This publication has been prepared jointly by ILO and ITDG, with funding support from the Swedish International Development Authority (SIDA).

ILO, ITDG and SIDA, together with CIDA, NORAD and SDC, are all supporting the International Forum for Rural Transport and Development (IFRTD) which was founded in 1991 and became operational in 1992. The Forum is a global initiative which aims to overcome the physical, social and economic isolation of the rural poor in developing countries. The overall objective of the Forum is to promote the implementation of transport systems which respond adequately to the needs of rural communities.

The Forum seeks to encourage greater recognition among policymakers and international development assistance agencies that improving access would reduce isolation and poverty; that the transport workload at the household level among poor rural communities is already onerous; and that without more effective and more efficient rural transport systems the ability of the rural poor to respond to or benefit from new social and economic development opportunities will continue to be highly restricted. The Forum aims to support governments, NGOs, donors, the private sector and other development institutions in responding to these rural transport issues.

This publication is intended to create awareness of, and disseminate information on, crucial rural transport issues. Further information about the Forum can be obtained from ILO or ITDG:

International Labour Organisation
E/DEV
CH-1211
Geneva 22
Switzerland

Intermediate Technology Development Group
Myson House
Railway Terrace
Rugby CV21 3HT, UK

1
Introduction

OVER THE LAST DECADE there has been increasing critical examination of, and debate about, the conventional approach to the research and planning of rural transport in developing countries. Studies in a variety of disciplines have indicated that roads and motor vehicles, which hitherto have been the central focus of transport models, have only a limited impact on many people living in rural areas. Transport analysts have increasingly come to the view that the 'highway-and-car' approach alone will not, in the foreseeable future anyway, be able to meet the totality of important transport demands of rural communities in the developing world.

Out of this debate has arisen a new approach to the analysis and understanding of rural transport patterns. The new approach questions the exclusive focus of conventional transport policies on improvements to and expansion of the current transport 'system', and calls for greater attention to examination of the real access needs of rural dwellers. The provision of transport facilities and services, it is argued, should be informed by the results of such an examination.

This publication has three objectives. The first is to trace the evolution of transport theory and policy and to chart the emergence of the new 'needs-led' approach. The second is to describe the methodology and findings of a number of recent studies which follow this approach. The third is to examine the implications of these findings for policymakers and to suggest a number of areas of intervention which could usefully be explored, to complement the development of rural road networks with a view to reducing the scale of the transport burden which currently imposes so heavily on the time and energy of the rural poor.

2
The evolution of rural transport theory and policy

HISTORICALLY, THE PATTERN of development of modern transport facilities in developing countries was stimulated and conditioned by a number of factors. Foremost among these was the need to facilitate and speed the journey of primary products to markets in Europe and North America. Additional functions of an improved transport network were the movement of food to growing urban centres and the establishment nationwide of judicial and administrative structures. In response to these needs, networks of highways and feeder roads, railways and ports were constructed, focusing on those areas which were most richly endowed with valuable primary commodities.

This pattern of transport infrastructure development has, in large measure, remained predominant since the Second World War. Continued dependence on the export of primary goods has necessitated heavy investment in transport facilities servicing this sector. In addition to the development of arterial connections serving resource-rich areas, however, road networks have also been expanded as national leaders have attempted to open up previously isolated and unexploited regions, to encourage economic development, and to link the nation together. For many developing countries, transport was the largest single sector for investment during the 1970s, with highway construction taking the lion's share.[1]

This strategy received strong support from international development assistance agencies, as evinced by their lending priorities. By the late 1970s, transport accounted for almost a quarter of World Bank loans and one-fifth of International Development Agency (IDA) credits (the soft-loan wing of the World Bank), ranking respectively first and second in their lending operations. Around half of the loans of both agencies in this sector went on roads and a third on railways.[1] Transport research was even more heavily weighted towards roads. It has been estimated that 94.5 per cent of World Bank funds targeted for transport research were devoted to this sub-sector.[2]

The mid-1970s marked the beginning of a shift in priorities and resources in developing countries away from major trunk roads towards expanding their networks of secondary and feeder roads. In part, this resulted from the view that in many countries the basic skeleton of transport infrastructure was already largely in place. However, it was also a response to the increased priority being attached to agricultural production and rural development. In this context, transport policies can be seen as having created, 'a polarized disharmony in which modern methods of transport are available, but only in limited areas and accessible to a minority of people'.[3] A number of studies showed that a significant proportion of the rural population lacked access to the road network.[4] In India, for example, a government survey found that 70 per cent of villages in the country did not have direct access to all-weather roads while 53 per cent were not connected to any road at all.[4] The resulting poor access of rural communities to their nearest supply depots, credit and extension services and markets was recognized as a heavy constraint on their productive potential.

Consistent with the general shift in priorities towards agriculture and rural development exemplified by Robert McNamara's presidency of the World Bank, resources were increasingly devoted to the construction of rural road networks. By 1977, 93 per cent of the total length of roads in projects funded by the World Bank were rural roads.[5] As part of the same process, the late 1970s also saw more interest on the part of the ILO, the World Bank and a number of bilateral aid agencies to use labour-based, rather than equipment-intensive, ways to build and maintain these roads. Such methods have the advantages of reducing the amount of foreign exchange spent; addressing the problems of equipment operation and maintenance in rural areas; and generating employment.

Limitations of the conventional rural transport model

Until the beginning of the 1980s, it was widely accepted that the motor vehicle – and with it the road and rail networks – provided the focus around which rural transport planning and policies would – and should – continue to be built. The ability of the

3

motorized road vehicle, and to a more limited degree the railway, to respond in an appropriate manner to transport needs in developing countries was largely taken for granted. 'There appears to be a fixed mind-set', noted Johnston in the context of south-east Asia, 'that sees the narrow, technical options of all-weather road and motor vehicle as the only feasible way of improving transport in the rural areas'.[6]

Continued public investment in the physical infrastructure for motorized vehicles, it was implicitly assumed, would eventually create an environment in which the transport needs of all would be more or less adequately catered for. This was perhaps nowhere more apparent than in Bangladesh. Despite the fact that non-motorized modes play a major role in the transport sector – in 1986 they accounted for 94 per cent of all commercially operated vehicles and two-thirds of total carrying capacity – only 0.004 per cent of all public investment in the transport sector had anything to do with non-motorized transport. In the words of one report, the transport policies of the government and aid agencies in Bangladesh 'effectively exclude 95 per cent of all vehicles and craft . . . [which] account for 75 per cent of the value added by transport operators'.[7] Further, investment in roads suitable for motorized vehicles in Bangladesh has had the effect of displacing many non-motorized operators from the market.

Over the last decade, however, the limitations of rural transport models which have focused more or less exclusively on roads and motor vehicles have increasingly been recognized. This has happened for a variety of reasons. In the first place, the poor economic performance of much of the Third World – particularly sub-Saharan Africa and poorer parts of Asia – during the 1970s and 1980s led to doubts about the ability of many countries to maintain their existing infrastructure, let alone to extend its range. A survey of 85 developing countries conducted by the World Bank in 1987 revealed that the backlog of economically warranted main road rehabilitation was some US$41 billion.[8] In addition, the severe foreign exchange shortages suffered by many countries restricted their ability to import vehicles and spare parts. In Ghana, for example, 70 per cent of the vehicle fleet was found to be inoperative in 1983 owing to a lack of imported spares.[9]

Another cause of the questioning of the 'conventional transport wisdom' was the emerging debate, and increasing lack of consensus, over the impact of rural roads on local communities: 'Our understanding of the means by which, and the circumstances under which, rural road projects influence economic development is less than complete.'[10] It had, for example, increasingly come to be recognized that there are a large number of variables at work other than the length of – and the level of access to – the road infrastructure. A study in Malawi, for instance, found that owing to a lack of vehicles in the country, the construction of an extensive road network had 'facilitated travel' but failed to 'induce greater mobility'.[11]

There was also considerable doubt as to who would be the primary beneficiaries of road investments. SEATAC[12] and Howe and Richards[13] both suggest that road investment could be unfair, by benefiting the 'richer of the poor' unless the balance was redressed by simultaneous investment in other sectors.

Similarly, Kaira pointed out that, particularly where there is monopolistic or oligopolistic control over trucking activities, the financial benefits of road construction will often accrue to traders rather than to the producers themselves.[2]

Other studies have also argued that the construction of roads has actually had ill effects such as displacing the operators of non-motorized modes of transport, as in the case of Bangladesh; encouraging the exodus of labour from the countryside into the cities;[14] or facilitating the flow of factory-produced goods into the rural areas, thus damaging local artisanal enterprises.[15]

Doubts were also expressed about how well motorized transport could be expected to accommodate the full range of transport needs in the rural areas. Researchers in a range of different disciplines – including agriculture, rural development, education, health and gender studies – found that, despite the increase in rural road networks, the great majority of rural dwellers continued to make little or no use of motor vehicles. These studies hinted at the existence of a significant transport burden in the rural areas which had hitherto been unrecognized by policymakers. The ILO studies conducted in Nigeria, India and Malaysia in 1981[16] were among the first to explore the scale of the time and load-carrying effort required for agricultural transport at the local level, away from the road network. Their conclusion that this constituted a major burden was mirrored by research conducted by Chambers et al.[17]

5

Kaira[2], Carr[18] and Curtis[19] also identified the existence of a significant transport burden for non-agricultural, domestic purposes such as the collection of water and firewood. A World Bank report estimated that in some rural African settlements, over one-quarter of some peoples' daily energy consumption was used in fetching water.[20] In practical terms, it was recognized that conventional transport modes would be inappropriate for such tasks.

The final reservation expressed about the ability of the motor vehicle to respond to the full range of transport needs was that, for certain transport tasks in the rural areas of developing countries, it might not be as cost-effective relative to traditional forms of transport as planners assumed. There were two elements to this argument. First, it was argued that a key assumption in official costing exercises, namely that motor vehicles operate at full load capacity, is rarely the case in rural areas: 'It was once thought that the use of antiquated carts which had survived centuries of change might not continue long in the era of motor transport. This expectation has not materialized because . . . due to insufficient loads, time taken in loading and unloading, long waiting at the market, the cost is so high that motor vehicles cannot as yet compete with the bullock cart. For conditions existing in the developing countries, the animal drawn vehicle is cheap for short hauls.'[21] Second, it was argued that calculations about the operating costs of motor vehicles omitted the costs of construction and maintenance of the road infrastructure necessary to support them. If these were included, it was claimed, non-motorized forms of transport might well prove to be more economical for certain transport functions.

By the mid-1980s, thinking on transport in developing countries was confused: there was little agreement on the role played by roads and motor vehicles or on their impact; the cost of maintenance of the road infrastructure was recognized as being unsustainably high; and, most seriously of all, large sections of the rural community were seen to be largely untouched by motorized vehicles. The key role of highways, motor vehicles and railways in the national social, economic and political life remained undisputed. Nevertheless, a growing appreciation of the scale of the transport burden at the local level for which, for the foreseeable future, the conventional transport system could

6

not fully cater, was provoking a reappraisal of the scope of transport policy.

It was out of this reappraisal that a new approach to rural transport analysis emerged in a series of studies, starting in 1986, conducted by specialist consultants IT Transport (UK) – in collaboration with ILO and other development agencies – in sub-Saharan Africa and in Asia. The studies sought to contribute to a better understanding of the real nature of rural transport needs, and to improve the effectiveness of rural transport policy-making and planning.

The new approach

The studies referred to above adopted a methodological approach different from that previously used for rural transport analysis. The central innovation was the introduction of the household (and the community of which it is a part) as the unit of analysis. Such an innovation had already been introduced into a number of other fields of study, most notably in the development of farming systems research. Even in the field of transport, the household had been used as the basis for appraising demand patterns in the industrialized countries since the mid-1950s, and somewhat later in the urban areas of some developing countries. No such methodology, however, had previously been introduced into rural transport analysis.

Data collection for the purposes of rural transport analysis had conventionally consisted principally of roadside surveys, involving interviews with vehicle owners and other road users. This method had several serious drawbacks. First, by restricting its scope to road users, most rural dwellers, who make little or no use of motorized transport, were to a large extent excluded from the transport planning process.[2] Second, it tended to over-value the importance of transport related to the production and marketing of cash crops (much of which takes place in bulk on the road network) at the expense of that related to small-scale crop marketing and subsistence tasks such as the collection of fire-wood and water. The result has been that much conventional transport research has provided a built-in rationale for the 'producer-surplus' approach to transport planning. In other words, the focus of attention on vehicles performing agriculture-related

7

tasks, operating on roads predominantly located in areas of high agricultural production, provides the justification for perpetuating existing trends in transport investment.

The new approach to rural transport analysis calls for a redefinition of rural transport, to be considered in its totality and to encompass: 'the movement of rural people and their goods to meet their domestic, economic and social needs, by any means, along paths, tracks and roads'.[10] This definition should, in fact, be extended to include waterways, an important component of the transport infrastructure in some countries. Rather than analysing the needs of the transport system from the point of view of a particular function to be performed, research should focus on a study of the transport needs of communities and of the individual households within them. In short, if the provision of transport services and facilities is to respond to the needs of people in the rural areas, planning must arise out of the measurement and understanding of just what those needs are.

As noted above, a number of studies in various disciplines had already thrown some light on the scale of the off-road transport burden. From the perspective of transport analysis, however, these studies had several weaknesses. First, since the focus of the research was rarely on transport itself, the data tended to refer to only one activity – such as water collection, visits to hospital or agricultural work – rather than to the totality of the households' transport movements. Second, where data on more than one transport activity were collected they were generally presented in a highly aggregated form, with little consideration taken for the relative importance of different activities. Third, many of the studies failed to distinguish between the work done by men and by women, with trips for domestic purposes often excluded from transport surveys, and women were infrequently interviewed since domestic work was excluded as a category of employment.[22]

While these studies in various disciplines succeeded in raising awareness about the importance of short-haul, non-motorized local trips both in creating agricultural surplus and in meeting basic subsistence needs, no fully comprehensive picture had emerged of the nature and scale of transport patterns; of the amount of time and effort spent on different tasks; of the relative importance of motorized and non-motorized forms of transport; of

8

the various methods and technologies used for different transport and travel functions; and of the degree to which transport constituted an impediment to enhanced health, welfare, income and total production.

It was this gap in knowledge which the series of studies initiated in 1986 sought to address by examining transport patterns at the community and household level. The findings of these studies are discussed in the next chapter.

3
The community-level studies

THE FIRST FOUR studies of rural household and community transport needs were carried out in early 1986 in Tanga Region of Tanzania; in 1986 and 1987 in Makete District of Tanzania; in late 1986 in Ghana; and in 1988 in Aurora Province of the Philippines. The studies in Tanga (for GTZ) and in Ghana (for the World Bank/Ministry of Transport and Communications) were undertaken by IT Transport as short-term consultancy assignments which imposed certain limitations on their scope. Those in Makete and Aurora, undertaken by IT Transport and ILO, had a more 'action-oriented research' approach, and hence were more comprehensive.

The methodology evolved and became more refined as the studies progressed. Nevertheless, the common aim of the studies was to quantify travel and transport characteristics and the data are suitable for comparative analysis (although those for Tanga are less comprehensive and less disaggregated than for the other study areas).

The four studies, therefore, range over conditions in east and west Africa and in south-east Asia. They are certainly much too limited in scope to be considered 'representative' of conditions in those regions. However, as the first studies to investigate rural household transport needs, their findings and insights are particularly valuable. Further studies are now under way, including detailed surveys as part of the Rural Travel and Transport Project of the World Bank's Sub-Saharan Africa Transport Programme, which will extend our understanding of rural transport.

Background characteristics of the study areas

Tanga Region is located in the north-east of Tanzania. The study comprised detailed surveys in six villages, selected to encompass the region's wide range of geographical and agricultural

10

conditions; of degrees of remoteness from the main road network and urban centres; and of different levels of access to social services and economic resources. The survey covered a total of 108 households.

Makete District is situated in the remote south-west of Tanzania, a poor highland area, with a lower population density and much lower growth rate than the national average, and most people living in scattered villages. The survey was conducted in 19 villages, selected to be representative of conditions in the district, and consisted of 431 household interviews.

Eight villages were surveyed in **Ghana** with a limited total sample of 51 household interviews. The villages were chosen to cover the three main physical and environmental zones in the country – the forest zone primarily in the centre and west, the coastal zone in the south and the northern savannah zone. Account was also taken of the villages' remoteness from urban centres, with a view to making them as representative as possible of conditions in each of the zones.

Aurora is a narrow, coastal province in the north-east of Luzon in the Philippines. Access to the province and within it is generally poor, with roads mostly in a deteriorated condition, many becoming impassable in the high-rainfall wet season. The province is bounded inland by a mountain range. The study was carried out in 22 rural communities with a total of 342 households being interviewed.

Methodology

A number of complementary research methodologies were used in each survey area. These were:

o structured discussions with village leaders and other key informants to obtain base data about the community and an over-view of its travel patterns, transport constraints and problems;

o questionnaire interviews with a random sample, generally 10 per cent, of households in each survey village to obtain data on the composition and economic characteristics of the households, on the transport elements of day-to-day activities in and around the village and on travel patterns outside the village;

o a simple mapping of each survey village to determine the

11

distances, and to define travel routes, to and from key facilities and access points within and around each village.

The most innovative element of the methodology was the collection, through the household interviews, of detailed data on travel patterns for all main trip purposes. Data were collected on trip frequency, trip time, means of transport used, load carried, and responsibility within the household for each of the following trip purposes:

Water collection
Firewood collection
Travel to the grinding mill
Supply of farm inputs
Crop production
Crop harvesting
Crop marketing
Travel to market
Travel to health facilities

Travel to market was treated separately from crop marketing since:

○ sale in a market is only one possible mechanism for marketing crops;

○ people travel to markets for many other reasons apart from crop marketing, for example, to buy food, household and consumer items, and for business and administrative purposes.

The findings of the studies

Distance to key places
The time needed for people to travel to a number of key facilities was measured for all of the areas. The findings are presented in Table 1. Distances are measured in terms of the average time required for a one-way trip to each of the facilities since this is the most fundamental indicator of accessibility.

Although significant variations were found, both within and between the study areas, the overall remoteness of people from the resources and facilities to which they need access was discovered to be considerable. The situation in Makete was the most severe, with household members having to travel for an average

12

Table 1. Average time required by households to reach selected facilities

Survey location	Water	Firewood	Cultivated land	Dispensary	Hospital	Grinding mill	Market
Tanga	31mins	44mins	N/A*	1hr 45mins	N/A	1hr 51mins	2hrs 37mins
Makete	23mins	1hr 38mins	1hr 5mins	1hr 36mins	5hrs 40mins	1hr 42mins	3hrs 18mins
Ghana	25mins	43mins	48mins	1hr 40mins	2hrs 38mins	28mins	2hrs 8mins
Aurora	5mins	27mins	11mins	25mins	1hr 54mins	21mins	2hrs 8mins

* Average figure not available. However 80 per cent of households have fields within a 30-minute walk.

13

of nearly 25 minutes to the nearest water source and for more than one hour to reach firewood 'and farm land. Very long journeys are required to reach the nearest dispensary, hospital, grinding mill and market. The situation is also severe in Tanga. On average, people have to walk for more than 30 minutes to reach a source of water. Access to sources of firewood and to markets, however, is better than in Makete.

While average travel times to most of the selected facilities were shorter in Ghana than in Makete, they were still sufficiently large to constitute a major transport burden for most households. Journeys of one hour and 40 minutes to the dispensary, two hours and 38 minutes to the hospital and more than two hours to the nearest market are particularly demanding.

Distances to many key facilities – particularly water, cultivated land and grinding mills – were much shorter in Aurora than in the African case studies. Nonetheless, journeys of two hours to both the hospital and the nearest market constitute a significant drain on the time available to most households.

Means of transport used
In each of the survey areas, the predominant means of travel was walking, with loads carried on the head or shoulder.

The most common vehicle is the bicycle. Some 28 per cent of surveyed households in Ghana owned a bicycle, with ownership being particularly common in the north of the country. While 29 per cent of households owned bicycles in Tanga, only one-third of these were in working order, suggesting a serious maintenance problem. In Makete, just over 6 per cent of households had bicycles in working order. Except in the north of Ghana, bicycles tend to be used only by men, primarily for short- and medium-distance trips outside of the village. The only other form of non-motorized transport in the African survey areas was a very small number of donkeys. These are used principally for the harvesting and marketing of crops.

A considerably greater range of non-motorized means of transport was identified at the local level in Aurora. Some 65 per cent of sampled households in Aurora owned a vehicle of some sort, the great majority being non-motorized. Almost half of the households owned a buffalo-drawn cart or sledge, while a quarter owned a bicycle, 10 per cent owned a boat and 5 per cent used a horse for transport purposes. None the less, as in the African study areas, the survey confirmed that the great bulk of personal travel and load-carrying around the village is done on foot. This is the predominant means of transport for the collection of water (93 per cent of households) and firewood (75 per cent of households). Non-motorized vehicles are, however, used more widely than in the African study areas for agricultural trips and for travel outside of the village. Sledges and carts are used by about 60 per cent of households for crop harvesting, and to a more limited extent for trips to the grinding mill, firewood collection, crop marketing and travel to the fields.

Ownership of motorized vehicles was extremely rare in all of the African study areas. The Ghana survey revealed a total of only 10 motor vehicles in the nine survey villages, with a population of over 21,000 people. In the Makete survey, with a population of approximately 13,700, only one household owned a four-wheeled motor vehicle, while three owned motor cycles. In Aurora a wider range of motorized vehicles was identified. These included power tillers with trailers (owned by 3.5 per cent of households), motor tricycles (1.8 per cent), tractors (1.5 per cent), jeeps (0.6 per cent), jeepneys* (0.6 per cent) and trucks (0.6 per cent).

The availability of motor vehicle services in each of the African survey areas was very limited. In Makete and Tanga, except for occasional bus services, the major role of motor vehicles is to provide transport services for government, church and medical personnel. A few lorries are also used but these tend to be employed for the collection of crops by marketing boards, and the distribution of building materials and fuel, rather than as a means of transport for rural people. In Ghana there are very limited motor vehicle services operated from either within or outside the villages and these cater predominantly for the needs of external marketing, journeys to hospital and social trips to other places. Motor vehicle journeys comprise a minute proportion of total household travel time.

In Aurora, motorized transport services are rather more common.

---

* The jeepney is an extended jeep, converted to carry passengers and accompanying goods. Jeepneys tend to operate on fixed routes, but not to a fixed timetable.

For personal travel and for load-carrying trips, the most commonly used transport service is provided by the motor tricycle. The survey found that this was used by 10 per cent of households for trips to the health centre, over 40 per cent for trips to hospital and 40 per cent for trips to market. Next in importance is the jeepney, followed by the *calesa* (horse-drawn cart) and the weapons carrier (a four-wheel-drive version of the jeepney). Buses are not used to any significant extent for load-carrying trips. Their use is essentially restricted to trips to health facilities, and long-distance personal travel beyond provincial boundaries, which is rare.

Travel patterns

Data were collected for the principal transport tasks of a sample of households in each of the survey areas. These data covered the purpose of each trip, the weight carried, the distance covered and the time taken. The data were analysed to provide a comprehensive picture of the transport burden involved in the achievement of the households' principal tasks, including the number of trips made; the total weight carried and the distance over which it was carried (expressed in terms of tonne-kilometres)*; and the time taken. The results were then disaggregated according to several criteria. First, the transport and travel patterns for internal purposes were compared with those for external purposes. Second, data were disaggregated in terms of each of the key transport tasks undertaken – the collection of water, trips to the grinding mill, etc. Third, the intra-family division of transport and travel activities was recorded.

The findings of the studies are summarized below according to each of these criteria in turn. A discussion of the data presented in this section should, however, be prefaced with a reminder that the figures quoted represent an average of the findings recorded for households in each of the study areas. While these aggregate

---

* Tonne-kilometre is the standard measure of the magnitude of any load-carrying transport activity: one tonne-km is the transport effort involved in the movement of a one-tonne load over a distance of one kilometre. In terms of walking trips carrying a 20kg load, one tonne-km equates to transporting 20kg over a distance of 50km. Note that transport effort was calculated only for those transport tasks that involved significant load-carrying.

figures do provide a useful 'broad-brush' picture, they often disguise significant variations within the samples. A more complete picture of conditions in the study areas can be obtained by consulting the original study reports.[23,24,25,26]

The aggregate transport burden
Details of the scale of the transport burden undertaken by rural households in the four study areas are presented in Table 2.

Table 2. Some indicators of the scale of the average transport burden undertaken by sampled households

	No. of Trips/Annum	Tonne-km/Annum	Time Spent/Annum
Tanga*	1,799	84.6	2,083 hours
Makete	1,772	86.5	2,475 hours
Ghana	4,224	216	4,832 hours
Aurora	1,914	92	736 hours

* The Tanga data excludes crop marketing, and trips to markets and health facilities.

The time and effort spent on transport can be seen to be substantial in each of the study areas. The 2,083 hours per annum devoted to transport tasks by households in Tanga understate the true scale of the burden in that a number of transport tasks outside the village – particularly marketing, and trips to market and to health facilities – were not analysed quantitatively in this survey. Nevertheless, even this reduced figure gives an average of 40 hours per week per household spent on transport, involving a workload of nearly 85 tonne-kilometres per annum.

The average of almost 2,500 hours per annum spent on transport by households in Makete represents nearly 50 hours per week, equivalent to more than a conventional full-time job for one person. The considerably higher figures recorded in the Ghana sample can be explained primarily by the larger average household size there. Sample households in Ghana had an average of 6.47 adults (3.08 women and 3.39 men), while those in Makete had an average of only 2.51 adults (1.34 women and 1.17 men).

The better access enjoyed by households in Aurora to key

17

facilities and to vehicles of various kinds means that the transport burden there is not so severe. Nevertheless, the time involved is about 750 hours per annum, equivalent to about 40 per cent of a conventional full-time job – or 15 per cent of the adult working time available to the typical household – and the annual workload equates to a transport effort of over 90 tonne-kilometres.

The relative importance of internal and external travel and transport
It was felt useful to disaggregate data for trips for internal and for external access. Internal access was defined as transport within the village, including the collection of water and firewood; trips to the field for crop establishment, weeding and harvesting; and marketing inside the village. External access was defined as travel outside the village, including journeys to health facilities and grinding mills, marketing outside of the village, and travel to places within and beyond the district. It is acknowledged that such a categorization results in certain anomalies. For example, some villages have grinding mills and health facilities which may be closer to some households than their supply of water or firewood. None the less, on the basis of the findings presented in Table 1 relating to the average distances between sampled households and selected facilities, the categories can be seen as valid.

Figures 1, 2 and 3 provide a comparison of the relative importance of internal and external travel – in terms of the number of trips, time spent, weight carried and tonne-kilometre transport effort in Makete, Ghana and Aurora respectively. Comparable data are not available from the Tanga study since some external tasks were not analysed quantitatively.

What is immediately apparent from these figures is the importance of internal travel and transport tasks as a drain on the time and energy resources of the average household relative to external travel in each of the study areas. Over 90 per cent of all trips are defined as internal, as is between 87 per cent and 96 per cent of the total weight carried in the three study areas. The relatively higher share of external travel in terms of time spent and tonne-km results from the longer trip distances involved. In Makete, travel to grinding mills and to markets account for the major part

18

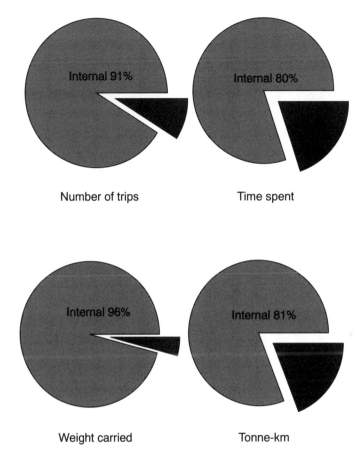

Internal 91%

Internal 80%

Number of trips

Time spent

Internal 96%

Internal 81%

Weight carried

Tonne-km

Figure 1. *Relative importance of internal and external travel in Makete District, Tanzania*

of external travel, while in Ghana and Aurora crop marketing and trips to market are most important. In the two African samples, 73 per cent or more of the time spent on transport, and of total transport effort, are devoted to the performance of internal transport tasks. In Aurora external travel is considerably more significant, reflecting greater integration into the cash economy.

19

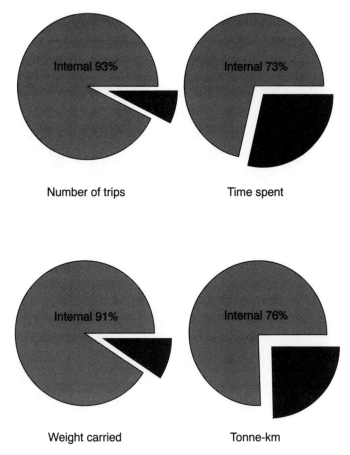

Number of trips   Time spent

Weight carried   Tonne-km

Figure 2. *Relative importance of internal and external travel in Ghana*

Disaggregation of household transport activities
In order to gain a more detailed understanding of the nature of the transport burden undertaken by households in the study areas, data were analysed at a considerably more disaggregated level to include the number of trips, time spent and tonne-kilometres for all of the principal transport activities, both internal and external. (In the case of Tanga, the data is partial since it excludes crop marketing, and trips to markets and health facilities.) Figures 4, 5, 6 and 7 provide a summary of this data.

20

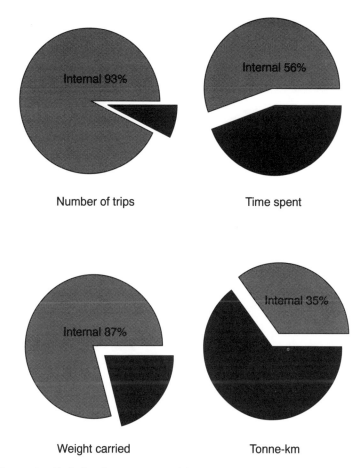

Number of trips   Time spent

Weight carried   Tonne-km

Figure 3. *Relative importance of internal and external travel in Aurora*

In each of the study areas water collection accounted for over 50 per cent of all trips. This task also accounts for nearly 50 per cent of transport time in Tanga and about a quarter of the total travel time in the other three study areas. This indicates that the transport of water tends to involve a large number of relatively short trips. Trip frequency for water collection was found to vary between 2.5 trips daily in Makete and up to six daily in Ghana (again reflecting larger household size in Ghana). Water transport constitutes a quarter or more of the total transport burden

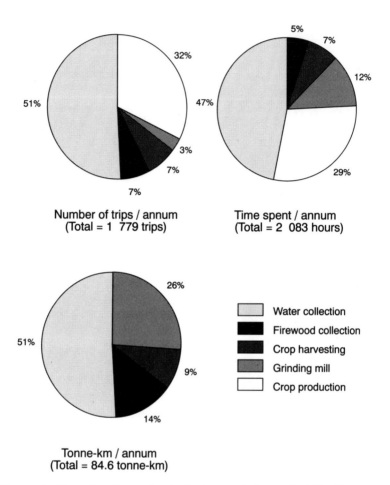

Number of trips / annum
(Total = 1 779 trips)

Time spent / annum
(Total = 2 083 hours)

Tonne-km / annum
(Total = 84.6 tonne-km)

Figure 4. *Travel pattern of a typical sample household in Tanga Region*

– in terms of tonne-kilometres – for typical households in Ghana, Makete and Tanga, confirming that the nearest water source is rather more distant than in Aurora where the transport of water constitutes only 10 per cent of the total transport effort.

The characteristics of firewood transport are rather different, with the percentage of both time spent and tonne-kilometre transport effort exceeding, in each of the study areas except Tanga, that of the number of trips made. This suggests a

22

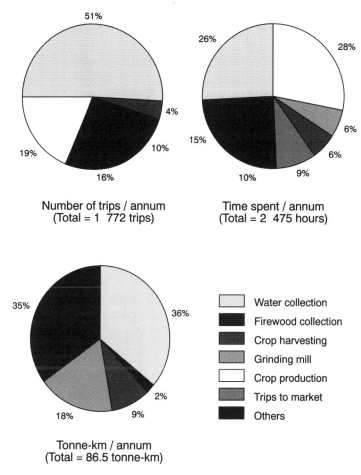

Number of trips / annum
(Total = 1 772 trips)

Time spent / annum
(Total = 2 475 hours)

Tonne-km / annum
(Total = 86.5 tonne-km)

Water collection
Firewood collection
Crop harvesting
Grinding mill
Crop production
Trips to market
Others

Figure 5. *Travel pattern of a typical sample household in Makete District*

relatively small number of journeys over longer distances. Trip frequencies were recorded at between 2.5 and 4.5 times per week. The collection of firewood is particularly onerous in Makete where it accounts for over 30 per cent of the total transport effort in terms of tonne-kilometres.

Transport related to visits to the grinding mill is of a similar nature in each of the study areas, with the percentage of time

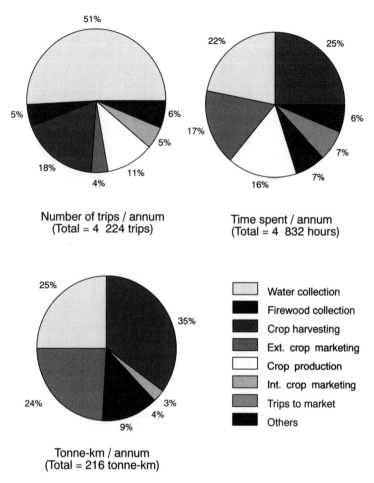

Number of trips / annum
(Total = 4 224 trips)

Time spent / annum
(Total = 4 832 hours)

Tonne-km / annum
(Total = 216 tonne-km)

Water collection
Firewood collection
Crop harvesting
Ext. crop marketing
Crop production
Int. crop marketing
Trips to market
Others

Figure 6. *Travel pattern of a typical sample household in Ghana*

taken and transport effort involved exceeding that of the number of trips. There is a significant difference between the study areas in terms of the relative importance of visits to the grinding mill; typical households in Ghana and Makete devoted 4 per cent and 18 per cent respectively of their total transport effort to this task. This may be explained principally by reference to cultural (particularly food preferences) and technological factors, with the processing of foodstuffs tending to be undertaken by the

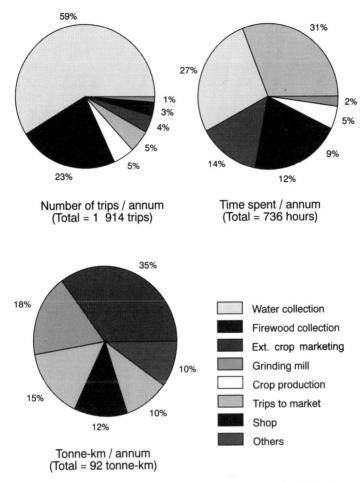

59%

27%

1%
3%
4%

5%

5%

23%

Number of trips / annum
(Total = 1 914 trips)

31%

2%

5%

9%

14%

12%

Time spent / annum
(Total = 736 hours)

35%

18%

10%

15%

10%

12%

Tonne-km / annum
(Total = 92 tonne-km)

☐ Water collection
■ Firewood collection
■ Ext. crop marketing
▨ Grinding mill
☐ Crop production
▨ Trips to market
■ Shop
▨ Others

Figure 7. *Travel pattern of a typical sample household in Aurora*

household itself in many parts of Ghana, while grinding of maize
at the mill is more common in Tanzania. The high proportion of
the tonne-kilometre transport effort devoted to visits to the
grinding mill (18 per cent) in Aurora relative to the number of
trips (1.2 per cent) and the time taken (2.2 per cent) is a consequence of the common use of vehicles to transport rice to the mill.

The importance of transport associated with crop production,
harvesting and marketing varies significantly between the study

25

areas. Journeys for crop production are considerably less time- and energy-consuming in Aurora than in the African study areas. This is due both to the agricultural system practised in Aurora (which requires less frequent visits to the fields) and to the easier access to farm land enjoyed by farmers there. In both Ghana and Makete, the proportion of time devoted to transport related to agricultural production is higher (16 per cent and 28 per cent respectively) than the number of trips (11 per cent and 18 per cent respectively), suggesting that farm land is generally at some distance from the household.

In Makete, the transport burden relating to crop harvesting is relatively small (only 6 per cent of total transport time and 9 per cent of transport effort), while that relating to crop marketing is insignificant. Since little produce is purchased by traders at the farm gate, the survey data suggest low levels of overall produc- tion and even lower levels of surplus production. Typical house- holds in Makete make an average of only 2.9 trips per annum for the purpose of external marketing. Crop harvesting transport in Makete, however, may have been underestimated. One of the food crops grown is cassava, which is 'stored in the ground' and harvested as required, often when people travel to the fields for other purposes. This task is therefore probably subsumed in the trips for crop production.

The harvesting and marketing of crops in Ghana, on the other hand, constitute a significant component of the household's total transport burden. The sample of households in Ghana included a large number which produce and market yams and cocoa. Harvest- ing accounts for 18 per cent of the trips made, 25 per cent of the total transport time and 35 per cent of the tonne-kilometre transport effort. The equivalent figures for external marketing are 4 per cent, 17 per cent and 24 per cent. These data describe a transport pattern characterized by the carrying of heavy loads over quite long distances, generally on foot.

It is most valuable to compare the harvesting and external marketing data for Ghana with those for Aurora. In Aurora non- motorized vehicles are used for harvesting, and motor vehicles for crop marketing. Thus, despite the fact that a higher proportion of the total tonne-kilometre transport effort is devoted to external marketing (35 per cent) than was the case in Ghana, the availability of vehicles means that only 0.13 per cent of trips and

1.5 per cent of transport time were devoted to the task. Similarly, the 5 per cent of total tonne-kilometres devoted to crop harvesting in Aurora was accommodated in only 1 per cent of trips and 0.9 per cent of total transport time.

It is important to note that, unlike most other transport tasks which are more or less evenly spread throughout the year, agriculture-related transport tasks tend to be seasonal in nature, peaking at certain periods in the farming calendar. Trips to the fields for land preparation, planting and weeding are required over a period lasting several months while harvesting and marketing necessitate a sharp increase in the scale of the transport burden for shorter periods. Households in areas such as the Ghana study areas, where a substantial amount of transport relating to crop harvesting and marketing is done by head-loading, see a major increase in transport activity then.

Visits to health facilities constitute only a small proportion (3.5 per cent or less) of the transport time in all of the study areas. Trips to market are also infrequent in Makete and Ghana, although they constitute a significant portion of the households' transport and travel time (9 per cent and 7 per cent respectively), confirming the finding that long distances need to be travelled to reach the nearest market. Visits to market constitute only 5 per cent of total trips in Aurora but 31 per cent of the typical household's transport time. This is explained by the long journeys which need to be made – an average of one and a quarter hours in the south of the province and two and a half hours in the north.

Household division of transport tasks
Data were also disaggregated by reference to the transport tasks undertaken by different members of the household. The findings for the Makete, Ghana and Aurora studies are presented in Figures 8, 9 and 10.

In both Makete and Ghana women shoulder a disproportionately large share of the transport burden. In Makete women are responsible for about 75 per cent of transport undertaken in terms of time taken and about 85 per cent in terms of tonne-kilometre transport effort. A similar picture emerges in Ghana where the typical woman devotes almost three times as many hours per annum to transport, and four times as much carrying effort, as the typical man.

27

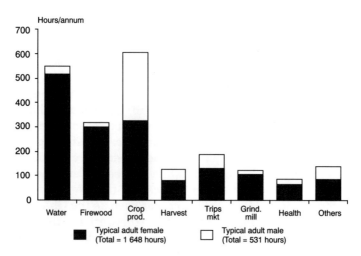

Figure 8(a). *Gender division of transport activities in Makete District (time spent)*

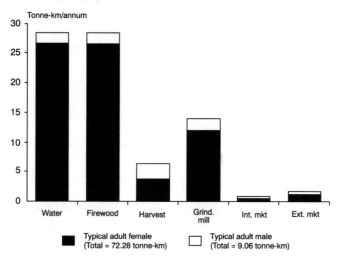

Figure 8(b). *Gender division of transport activities in Makete District (tonne-km)*

In both countries women, assisted by their children, take predominant responsibility for the collection of water and firewood and for trips to the grinding mill. Women contribute more labour to every transport task for which data were collected in

28

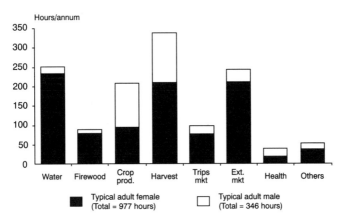

Figure 9(a). *Gender division of transport activities in Ghana (time spent)*

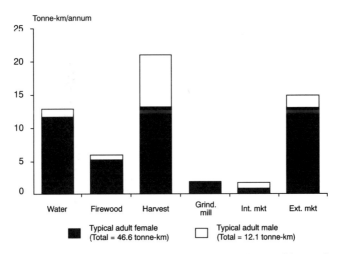

Figure 9(b). *Gender division of transport activities in Ghana (tonne-km)*

Makete, devoting about 60 per cent of the transport time required for crop production, nearly 70 per cent of the transport time for crop marketing, and 60 per cent of the transport time for harvesting. In Ghana the intra-household share of the transport burden is slightly more equal, with men sharing approximately equally the

29

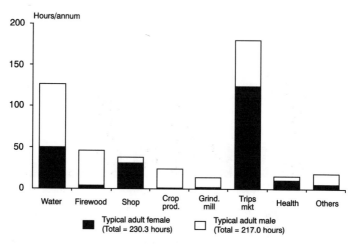

Figure 10(a). *Gender division of transport activities in Aurora (time spent)*

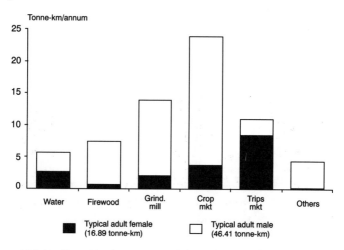

Figure 10(b). *Gender division of transport activities in Aurora (tonne-km)*

transport tasks associated with crop establishment and internal crop marketing. Women are primarily responsible for all other transport tasks, including an approximate 90 per cent share of the transport burden associated with external crop marketing which is a major consumer of time and energy.

These data describe a major transport burden to be borne by women in the African study areas which was also reflected in the Tanga survey. The typical able-bodied woman in the Makete study area spends about 1,650 hours per annum, that is over 30 hours every week or over four hours per day, solely on transport. In Ghana, the typical female spends around 1,000 hours per annum or nearly 20 hours weekly on transport. These figures constitute the equivalent of 80 per cent and 50 per cent respectively of the time a typical worker would expect to devote to a conventional full-time job, and must be undertaken in addition to the many other domestic duties for which women take principal responsibility. The typical adult male in Makete and Ghana devotes respectively about 10 hours and seven hours each week to transport.

The full magnitude of the transport burden undertaken by women becomes yet more apparent when one takes into account the seasonal nature of the transport burden associated with agriculture. During the harvesting and marketing seasons, womens' transport workloads are considerably greater than the average described above.

A very different picture emerges in the case of Aurora. Adult males take the greater responsibility for transport tasks and contribute about 50 per cent of the time devoted by the household to transport and 75 per cent of the total transport effort.

The wider picture

The survey findings portray a transport burden whose existence may have been recognized in general terms, but the scale and nature of which has hitherto been little appreciated, and has not been quantified. Transport research and planning, as noted earlier, have been largely focused on the needs of agricultural marketing and long-distance, motorized, personal travel, with investment heavily weighted towards rural road infrastructure development. The surveys reveal that this approach does not address the totality of important rural transport needs:

o to a greater or lesser extent, tasks relating to the meeting of subsistence needs in the four study areas outweigh those relating to agricultural production and marketing;

31

o only a small fraction of the journeys made by rural people are outside the locality of their home village. Such journeys are rare in all of the study areas.

This is not, of course, to argue that rural roads are unimportant: motor vehicle access to the rural areas is essential for moving marketed crops; for the distribution of agricultural inputs such as fertilizer and seeds; and for the delivery of economic and social services. Motor vehicle access is also important in facilitating use of more centralized services such as hospitals; and in allowing longer-distance personal travel for social, educational, employment and business purposes. The fresh insight offered by the study findings is that, beyond the scope and concern of conventional transport planning, there exists an unacknowledged, local level (and often off-road) rural transport burden of major proportions.

This insight is significant from several points of view. First, it sheds fresh light on the scale of the drudgery of rural life in many parts of the developing world and on the implications that poor access to facilities, services and goods has for the welfare of the people living there. Second, it raises questions about the degree to which rural populations have the capacity to increase agricultural production in line with the farm models used by development planners in promoting 'improved' practices, given that household labour is an important factor of production.

It is clearly prudent to be cautious in drawing generalized conclusions from the community-level studies. The number of studies undertaken to date is small, and there are variations in findings both between and within the study areas. The differences between the findings of the African studies and the Asian study are particularly pronounced in this respect.

There is, however, considerable supporting evidence to suggest that the overall picture which emerges from the studies – of a heavy and arduous transport burden borne by rural households – forms part of a wider pattern. This evidence is of two types: firstly, in addition to the Aurora study reported here a few other studies of household transport patterns have been undertaken in recent years in various parts of Asia, and; secondly, studies from a variety of different disciplines have generated findings which are complementary to and broadly supportive of the community-level studies.

Other studies of rural household transport patterns in Asia
Three of the four community-level studies discussed above as well as much of the complementary evidence which follows below, relate to Africa. In a region with as diverse a range of cultural, geographical and economic conditions as exists in Asia, few general conclusions about rural transport characteristics could be drawn on the basis of only one comprehensive transport study. It is undoubtedly true that additional research is required in Asia into the nature and scale of the rural transport burden. Specifically, there is a need to improve our understanding of:

○ the circumstances under which, and the ways in which the scale of the rural transport burden constrains economic and social development;

○ the variations in allocation of responsibility for transport tasks between men and women, and the situations where the burden of transport falls unduly on women and inhibits them from making a greater contribution to productive and welfare activities.

None the less, the availability of additional recent household-level research from Asia allows us to discuss transport characteristics more widely in the region with a little more confidence. The findings of three recent studies of rural transport patterns – in the Philippines, Indonesia and Laos – will be discussed in turn.

Following the completion of the work in Aurora, similar studies were conducted in two provinces of the northern Philippines.[27,28] The majority of the land area in both provinces is hilly or mountainous terrain. The findings from these studies were broadly similar to those from Aurora. The following findings are worth highlighting:

○ ownership of motor vehicles was very rare. Ownership of non-motorized means of transport, and access to motor vehicle transport services was lower than Aurora. This reflected the terrain conditions and resulted in a higher dependence on travel by foot;

○ the total time spent on transport was significantly higher than in Aurora, but still lower than in the African study areas, at about 1,250 hours per annum. About 80 per cent of this time was spent on internal transport within the community. Water and firewood collection, and trips to the market, were the

33

most time-consuming transport tasks. The major load-carrying effort was for water and firewood collection, travel to the rice mill, transport of fertilizer and crop marketing.

A study of 20 villages was carried out in Indonesia in 1988.[6] Thirty per cent of the sample villages had all-weather road access, 30 per cent dry-season road access, and 40 per cent no direct road access. Motor vehicle ownership was restricted to 0.6 per cent of the households surveyed. The study analysed the significance of walking trips, with the following results:

○ walking trips accounted for more than 60 per cent of all trips in every village, and more than 80 per cent of all trips in 16 out of the 20 villages;

○ in 12 out of the 20 villages, more than 60 per cent of the total weight of goods transported was carried on foot;

○ in 16 out of the 20 villages, more than 60 per cent of the total time spent on transport was devoted to walking trips. This was the case in five of the six villages with all-weather road access.

A small household study of three villages in Champasak province in the People's Democratic Republic of Laos was carried out as one element of a much larger national transport study.[29] The three villages were selected to represent different levels of road access in an area where the transport situation was regarded as 'above average', but income was about 30 per cent below the national average. No household owned a motor vehicle, 3 per cent had bicycles, and 6 per cent elephants. Relevant findings are summarized below:

○ the communities had good access to facilities in the village: 97 per cent of households within 500m (7–8 minutes walk) of a source of water; rice fields generally within 2km (about a 30-minute walk) of the house; all households within 2km of a school;

○ only trips longer than 1km were analysed: of these 62 per cent were to the field, 17 per cent to collect firewood, and most of the remainder to other places within 15–20km. The average household made only 0.07 trips per year outside the province, and 10 trips per year to the district/province centre. Households only visited the market 3–6 times per annum;

o travel within and around the village was predominantly on foot. Walking was also important for travel outside the village. For example, about 90 per cent of households walked for 6–20km to catch a bus to market.

The findings from the Philippines, Indonesia and Laos indicate a better level of access to facilities in the village (for example, sources of water) than is the case in Africa, and this would be expected to reduce the total time and effort devoted to transport. However the data are too fragmented to permit generalizations for the whole of Asia. The sum of the evidence from Asia suggests a continuing significant dependence on walking to meet transport needs. The extent of this dependence, particularly for agricultural trips and travel outside the village, appears to relate to the level of ownership of non-motorized means of transport, and the availability of transport services. However the need for further research on local-level rural transport in Asia remains.

Complementary evidence
As noted above there is a body of complementary evidence which is broadly supportive of the findings of the community-level studies. Recent research in sub-Saharan Africa, for example, has confirmed that walking is much the most common transport mode. Traffic counts made at 55 points on rural roads in Uganda found that of an average 715 recorded journeys per day, 75 per cent were made by pedestrians, 22 per cent by bicycles and only 2 per cent by motor vehicles.[30] A study in Kenya, meanwhile, found that 70 per cent of all journeys in the rural areas were made on foot, 7 per cent by public transport and 2 per cent by private motor vehicle.[30]

A similar picture emerges from studies conducted in Asian countries. Traffic counts conducted on 78 rural roads in Bangladesh, for example, found that motor vehicles and motor cycles accounted for, respectively, only 1 per cent and 5 per cent of all traffic. Pedestrians accounted for 46 per cent and non-motorized vehicles 47 per cent of all recorded journeys.[31] Surveys conducted in Nepal, where two-thirds of the population live in the hills where roads are few, found that, in the Kosi Hill area, on certain sections of the foot trails more than 500,000 trips per year – 1,350 trips per day – are made.[32]

35

A number of empirical studies have also confirmed the findings of the community-level studies that most of the transport of goods in rural areas is undertaken by head-loading. Research in Ghana found that for more than 90 per cent of households surveyed, the principal means of carrying goods from farming land was by head.[30] Another recent study in Ghana revealed that 38 per cent of the weight of commodities carried on the more than 200 rural roads studied was by head-loading, with the proportion rising to up to 90 per cent on roads carrying less than 25 vehicles per day.[30] Research in rural India found that 81 per cent of the total weight of goods transported was carried on trips inside the village, much of which was undertaken by head-loading.[33] The survey in the Kosi Hills of Nepal found that over 6,000 tonnes of goods per year are carried in the hills by head on the foot trails.[32]

The particularly heavy transport burden shouldered by women in the African study areas has been mirrored by the findings of a number of other studies. A World Bank study found that in certain parts of Sudan the time needed to fetch fuelwood has increased more than fourfold between the mid-1970s and the mid-1980s. The study also found that in parts of the continent mothers are taking their daughters away from school to help them gather fuel, and that time is increasingly being diverted to this task from other pressing priorities such as timely planting and weeding, and child care. The study concluded that 'available evidence suggests a widespread phenomenon of increasing pressure on women's time'.[34]

Several researchers have suggested that the scale of the transport burden undertaken by women may be a factor inhibiting agricultural output in Africa. 'There is evidence that reliance on headloading (which is predominantly a female activity) is a significant constraint on small-farm output in Ghana.'[35] A recent ILO report came to a similar conclusion without making specific reference to transport: '[African] women are, in general, overworked in the rural areas and . . . pressure on women's time is an important constraint on raising agricultural production and rural living standards'.[36]

In this respect it is important to recognize that transport is a 'derived' need. It is an essentially unproductive activity which is only carried out in order to meet other needs. If the transport burden were reduced, household labour resources would be released for other more productive, or socially beneficial, activities. It is also important to recognize the extensive nature of agriculture in much of Africa (the modest increases in agricultural production in Africa – no more than 2 per cent per annum during the last three decades – have derived mostly from an expansion in the area under cultivation rather than from increases in yields and productivity).[37] Further increases in output would be likely to involve a further extension of agriculture, implying greater trip distances to reach farming land and to transport the harvest.

In Asia, too, there is reason to believe that transport volumes are set to grow significantly in coming years. The increasing emphasis on agricultural diversification allied with the more widespread dissemination of high-yielding varieties and official efforts to develop rural-based agro-industries in much of the continent are all likely to add to the transport workload.[33]

Conclusion

In conclusion, both the household surveys and a number of other recent transport studies identify the existence of a substantial transport burden to be undertaken by rural households, predominantly off the road network and on foot. In addition, a body of complementary research not specifically focused on transport indicates that growing time constraints on rural households – and particularly on women in Africa – may be inhibiting their ability to increase agricultural output.

By measuring the scale and describing the nature of the transport burden, the community-level studies serve a dual purpose:

o they provide an understanding of the share of transport tasks in the total labour effort made by rural households and by the different members within them;

o they help to identify the different tasks which contribute most heavily to the overall transport burden, thus enabling policy to be formulated in such a way as to tackle the key transport bottlenecks and constraints.

Rural transport as a system has been much neglected in many parts of the Third World with the result that transport facilities and services, as presently constituted, frequently bear little

37

relation to the totality of the needs of rural communities. In consequence, a substantial amount of time and energy must be devoted to transport and is drained away from potentially more productive or welfare-enhancing activities. There is, however, a wide range of policy instruments – much wider than has generally been employed to date – available to address this problem. The next chapter is given over to an examination of these instruments.

4
Towards more appropriate rural transport policies

THE COMMUNITY-LEVEL studies do not offer a complete picture of rural transport characteristics and problems in the developing world. None the less, as a result of these studies, much of value can now be said about the problems associated with rural transport and the measures which can be taken in response to those problems. There is a growing body of experience and research from the developing world relating to measures aimed at alleviating the rural transport burden. While this confirms the high level of diversity of conditions both within and among regions and countries, it also reveals a considerable degree of shared experience, with certain policies working to good effect in different areas and conditions.

The scope of rural transport policy

The foregoing analysis implies that conventional policies are not addressing effectively the full range of transport requirements of rural communities in developing countries, and that the fundamental reason for this is that policies are too narrowly focused. The foremost need is for a thorough reappraisal of the role and scope of policy in the realm of rural transportation. This reappraisal should involve three key developments in strategic thinking.

○ Recognition that the range of initiatives and policies which could be adopted is considerably greater than has generally been exploited to date. For example, efforts to enhance off-road mobility could include the introduction and promotion of non-motorized modes of transport other than head-loading and, in many cases, the development of the footpath network.

○ Broadening of the definition of the problem beyond 'mobility' to encompass the wider concept of 'accessibility'. In other

39

words, the core problem should be seen as the scale and nature of the transport task rather than the inadequacy of the transport system *per se*. This apparently semantic point does, in fact, have important policy implications. It opens the door not just to policies to improve people's mobility by making transport faster, less burdensome and cheaper, but also to those which reduce or obviate the need to travel, generally by the location of facilities and the delivery of services and goods closer to rural communities.

○ Acknowledgement that policies appropriate to reducing the rural transport burden must be location-specific. That they must, in other words, respond more closely to the specific physical, cultural and socio-economic characteristics and needs of the target area. Such an approach has recently been proposed by Johnston in the context of south-east Asia.[6] Calling for a move away from 'project-based planning' towards 'area-based planning' methods, he calls for a more open-minded and imaginative response to rural transport which takes local factors into account.

These shifts in perspective imply a radical reorientation of the focus of policy in relation to rural transport. First, they suggest that the scope of policy to enhance the mobility of rural people and their goods should be extended beyond rural road infrastructure. This is not to say that roads are not deserving of continuing attention. It is, rather, to recognize that complementary measures are required for the more effective functioning of the entire transport network: 'Full utilisation of (a feeder road) will, to a great extent, depend on the local transport system feeding it.'[2] The transport demands of rural households, as identified in the community-level studies, indicate two broad categories of need for enhanced mobility. First, the need to be able to transport relatively small loads over relatively short distances and sometimes over difficult terrain. Second, the need to make less frequent, but longer journeys (of people and goods) to facilities such as markets and hospitals. There are three ways in which the mobility of rural households can be enhanced, to address these needs:

○ greater use of intermediate means of transport;

○ development of local transport infrastructure;

○ expansion of local rural transport services.

The shifts in perspective imply, however, that the scope of rural transport policy should not be limited to measures to enhance mobility. Policy should also encompass measures to reduce the need for travel and transport, primarily by locating facilities and services closer to the communities that need access to them. Enhanced mobility, and provision of services and facilities, may be regarded as the two complementary elements of a comprehensive rural transport policy. This in turn leads to the need for recognition of the fact that the range of possible interventions to address the rural transport burden are complementary rather than competitive, and are likely to be most effective when applied in an integrated manner. This signals a move towards area-based planning, identifying the appropriate mix and balance of interventions to address location-specific rural transport needs.

This chapter examines the range of options to address the rural transport problem. It deals first with the three types of measure to enhance rural mobility. It then examines the scope for reducing the need for travel and transport. Finally it considers the complementarity of different types of intervention, and the potential for area-based planning. The chapter illustrates policy options with examples of measures which have been successfully introduced in different developing countries.

Intermediate means of transport

There exist in different parts of the developing world low-cost vehicles and carrying devices of various kinds which have proved appropriate to local-level transport tasks. These are collectively called intermediate means of transport (IMTs) – intermediate, that is, between walking (with loads carried on the head) and conventional, expensive and high-capacity motor vehicles.

IMTs include:

o simple devices to facilitate the carrying of loads by people, such as the shoulder pole and the 'chee-geh' back frame used in the mountainous regions of Korea;

o human-powered vehicles such as wheelbarrows, handcarts and the ubiquitous bicycle, sometimes equipped with a trailer or other means of increasing its load-carrying capacity;

41

o animal-powered devices – donkeys with panniers, animal-drawn carts and sledges;

o low-cost motorized vehicles such as the moped (mobylette) and the motor cycle (sometimes with a sidecar or trailer) used for local-level transportation in some rural areas in Asia and in francophone west Africa, and simple vehicles powered by single-cylinder diesel engines;

o boats, propelled by oars, sails or small motors, used in river and coastal areas.

These IMT share a number of advantages over conventional motor vehicles for local-level rural transport tasks:

o they are considerably cheaper;

o they are better suited to small-scale, decentralized manufacture;

o they require a lower level of maintenance and/or are easier to maintain relying on locally available materials and skills;

o they are more suited to the small- and medium-sized loads which often need to be transported at local-level. They do, none the less, significantly increase the size of loads and/or the speed (and hence range) of travel compared with head-loading. Field studies in northern Ghana have found that, if speed and payload are taken into account, the bicycle trailer can increase a person's transport capacity by at least five times;[30]

o they can operate on a more rudimentary and inexpensive physical infrastructure. Even large IMT such as animal carts need only a reasonably flat surface about two metres wide, while bicycles, or donkeys with panniers, need only a well-trodden path.

In a world of scarcity, the principal advantage to the rural household of the cheap, low-capacity vehicle over the conventional motor vehicle is quite simply that it is more likely to be available, affordable and usable.

The value of IMTs in rural areas is testified to both by the number of places where they have evolved spontaneously, and by the positive impact they have had in those areas. The Aurora study identified the presence of significant numbers of IMTs as one key reason why the transport burden on individuals there was considerably less onerous than in the African study areas. Other examples of IMTs playing a key role in enhancing agricultural output and alleviating the drudgery associated with rural transport abound: the 'scotchcart', drawn by either oxen or donkeys, which has played a central role in the growth of smallholder productivity in Zimbabwe since independence; the bullock cart, common in many areas, but perhaps most strongly associated with rural India; and the bicycle, which enhances mobility and provides improved carrying capacity for millions of households throughout the developing world.

The fact that IMTs have evolved through commercial initiatives, often with little or no state intervention, does not mean that there is no need for outside support and assistance to the sector. There are many areas where few or no IMTs are to be found. As one example, there appears to be substantial potential in Africa for the dissemination of greater numbers of animal-drawn carts. Only 10 per cent of African farmers who own draft animals also have a cart,[38] while, with a population of around half that of India, Africa has only around one-twentieth as many animal carts (700,000 against 15 million).

Strong constraints exist to the development and dissemination of low-cost vehicles. The adoption of appropriate policies and measures by governments, NGOs and development assistance agencies would contribute to addressing these constraints, and to stimulating a greater use of IMTs. Such policies and measures fall under four general categories:

○ education and awareness;
○ production and supply;
○ affordability;
○ import policy.

Education and awareness
There is in many places, particularly in Africa, a general lack of awareness about IMTs. Certainly there is a lack of awareness about the full diversity of types of IMT that exist and are used successfully in different parts of the developing world, and about the benefits that they can offer to rural people. This lack of awareness exists at two levels: among policymakers and among potential IMT users.

Among policymakers, IMTs are often regarded as 'primitive',

43

'backward', or as being at best temporary palliatives which will rapidly be superceded by 'modern' motor vehicles. This lack of acceptance of their legitimacy and continuing significance and relevance has tended to result in their being overlooked in policy-making.

A lack of awareness about IMTs among rural dwellers in many areas also acts as a serious constraint on their wider dissemination. If farmers have never seen oxen drawing a cart, or a bicycle pulling a trailer, they are unlikely to appreciate the vehicles' benefits and, as a result, are unlikely to articulate a demand for the devices.

Governmental bodies, development programmes and NGOs can perform an educational role in creating awareness of, and demonstrating the value of, IMTs in the rural areas. This is a particularly valuable function when allied to initiatives which promote the supply of the vehicles being demonstrated. One way in which organizations can increase the awareness of rural communities about the value of IMTs is by using the vehicles in their own rural extension activities. This has been demonstrated by the Forestry Department in Andra Pradesh, India, which uses cycle trailers for local-level load-carrying tasks. IMTs can prove highly appropriate for many rural extension activities.

It should, however, be recognized that education and awareness-raising are part of a long-term process. Cultural attitudes, such as the reluctance of traditional cattle-owning societies in Africa to work their animals, or the inhibitions about women riding bicycles, can be changed but the process can take time.

Production and supply

Small, rural enterprises can manufacture certain types of IMT if they have access to the necessary materials and equipment. Small-scale rural manufacture has certain advantages:

○ the production methods and schedules are suited to the uneven nature of the demand which will often exist for IMTs – this often relates to the agricultural cycle;

○ small-scale, local enterprises can respond to specific requirements in different locations;

○ maintenance and repair capability is locally available;

○ distribution costs are low;

○ it advances the process of rural industrialization, a goal pursued by an increasing number of governments. India goes so far as to restrict the manufacture of animal carts to small workshops.[33]

There is great scope for assistance by governments and NGOs to the small-scale production sector – in improving access to materials and credit; in introducing new products; in introducing new techniques for the manufacture of parts whose limited availability causes a bottleneck in the production process; or in enhancing the quality of devices already being produced. Even in countries where small-scale producers are already making functional IMTs, there is generally considerable scope for the introduction of simple, efficient technologies and production techniques which will improve the devices' performance and/or reduce their cost. Box 1 provides an example of one such innovation – a hand-operated machine enabling small-scale producers to make a variety of types and diameters of wheel – which has been adopted by artisanal animal-cart producers in several countries.

Small-scale, decentralized production of IMTs can be supported and promoted by the import, or centralized manufacture, of certain complex and critical components. Artisan producers are rarely able to manufacture such components as efficient bearings, pneumatic tyres and inner tubes. In some countries, such components may be available at prices affordable to the vehicle purchaser, either new or as scrap/second-hand parts. However, where such components are scarce or expensive, governments can adopt policies to encourage larger local companies to establish manufacturing capacity. In India, for example, a company set up production of low-cost pneumatic tyres suitable for bullock carts. The Chinese government established capacity for the manufacture of ball bearings, axles, wheel components and pneumatic tyres to enable local rural producers to improve the quality of traditional wheelbarrows, handcarts and animal carts.[33] Such interventions simultaneously improve the supply of necessary components to artisanal producers and reduce foreign-exchange expenditures.

In countries where there is a fairly high and regular demand for IMTs, large-scale, central production may be more appropriate. In Burkina Faso, for example, demand for a wide range of agricultural equipment, including ox and donkey carts, is sufficiently high, and predictable – because, as part of agricultural development policy there are national credit schemes for small farmers – to make centralized, large-scale production of carts feasible and efficient. Costs of distributing carts to rural purchasers are kept low by distributing them as kits to be assembled in rural

46

centres. Similar schemes operate in some other African countries including Togo and Mozambique.[38]

The manufacture of complete bicycles is, for technical reasons, only likely to be viable on a large-scale. Governments can adopt policy measures to facilitate the establishment of bicycle production. The governments of both India and China adopted strategies of gradually developing indigenous bicycle manufacture, beginning with the assembly of imported components and progressively increasing local content until full domestic manufacture was achieved. The relatively small domestic markets in most African countries mean that bicycle production is likely to have a lower local content, and will often need to serve regional rather than purely national markets. The Peugeot bicycle factory in Burkina Faso, for example, sells to neighbouring countries.

There are examples from Latin America of NGOs supporting the development of domestic bicycle production capacity. The US-based group, Bikes Not Bombs, has shifted the focus of its activities away from the donation of bicycles from its supporters in the US towards the setting up of a bicycle assembly industry in Nicaragua. The Centre for Appropriate Technology in El Salvador (CESTA), has obtained start-up funds necessary for bicycle assembly facilities.[39]

Thus there are options for the scale of production of IMT. Full production of bicycles is essentially large-scale, but they can be assembled, and even some components manufactured, on a smaller scale. For IMT such as carts, barrows, trailers, etc., the options range from large-scale centralized manufacture to small-scale rural production. Different scales of production may address different demands. In Zimbabwe, for example, large- and small-scale producers of animal carts co-exist, with the former marketing in areas of high agricultural production where demand is high and relatively predictable – in that many of the orders are placed via the Agricultural Finance Corporation (AFC) which provides credit for cart purchase – while artisanal producers are more active in the poorer south where demand is lower and somewhat more sporadic. The key need is that governments adopt the range of policies to facilitate, and encourage, manufacture of different types of IMT at the appropriate scales to meet different demands.

47

Affordability

A critical issue in the dissemination of IMTs is that of afford-ability. Some simple carrying devices, such as animal sledges crafted from tree trunks, may have minimal or zero monetary cost, but such devices tend to be relatively inefficient and to have limited carrying capacity and/or speed. The acquisition of most IMTs, particularly those characterized by a significant enhancement in carrying capacity and/or speed relative to head-loading, involves a monetary investment. While this cost is considerably less than that of conventional motor vehicles, it nonetheless represents a very substantial investment for many – or even most – rural households.

Clearly, it is difficult to generalize about this since there is a wide diversity both in the cost of the various IMTs and in the purchasing power of rural households in different countries in the developing world. Nevertheless, purchasing power in many rural regions is low, and has been adversely affected by disappointing economic performance and the policies of structural adjustment. In many developing countries the retail price of the IMTs on the market is equivalent to a high proportion of the average annual household income. The cost of animal carts in Zambia and Tanzania – where per capita GNP (1990) is, respectively, US$420 and US$110 – ranges between US$150 and US$450. In Malawi, which has a per capita GNP of US$200, animal carts cost up to US$1,000.[40] Bicycles can be bought in Tanzania for between US$77 and US$120 and in Burkina Faso (per capita GNP US$330) for around US$210.

Thus, even though IMT are 'low-cost' in comparison with conventional motor vehicles, they are expensive in relation to the incomes of many rural households. At first sight this would seem to imply that ownership of IMT is beyond the means of most rural households, and that the benefits from their use will accrue only to richer households who are able to afford them. That this is not the case is because of two factors. First, there is considerable evidence from areas where IMT (and particularly animal carts) are used at present, that the majority of households who benefit from their use gain access to IMTs not by ownership, but rather by hiring the vehicles, or by borrowing them from relatives, when required. Thus, the ownership of animal carts by a few (often richer) households in a community can contribute to alleviating transport problems for many people in the area. Second, there are examples from developing countries where the provision of credit facilities has stimulated the purchase by rural households of IMTs. The importance of credit reflects the fact that, while many rural households do not have sufficient cash to buy an IMT, the financial return from ownership can be high. Even in such a relatively fertile and wealthy area as Mashonaland, Zimbabwe, the widespread dissemination over the last decade of ox-carts has been to a significant degree dependent on the provision of credit by the Agricultural Finance Corporation (AFC). Conversely, in areas where such credit facilities are not available, IMT dissemination has proved much more difficult. Programmes to promote the use of animal-drawn carts in the relatively prosperous western highlands of Kenya, for example, have run up against the problem of the inability of all but a few farmers to make the necessary monetary investment without some assistance.

In areas of some agricultural potential, there is substantial scope for the establishment of credit facilities. Farmers should be able to generate enough extra earnings as a consequence of IMT ownership – through increased agricultural production and/or hire of the vehicle – to repay the cost comfortably. A recent study in western Kenya found that in most areas, many farmers would be able to repay credit for the purchase of an animal-drawn cart within one farming season.[41] Credit schemes of this type are already in operation. Banks in India have for several years been financing the purchase of bullock carts for farmers producing crops for the jute and sugar industries. Cotton farmers in the south-west of Burkina Faso have access to substantial credit facilities, provided by the state, for the purchase of all types of agricultural equipment, including vehicles such as animal carts, bicycles and motor cycles. Credit facilities can be provided by private companies involved in vehicle distribution. In the Philippines, motor cycles and side-cars, known as tricycles, are marketed by motor cycle dealers. The most common form of sale is on a hire-purchase basis, with full payment made over an 18-month or two-year period.

Under certain conditions credit schemes to help even the poorest households to purchase IMTs may prove sustainable. The Grameen Bank in Bangladesh, which makes small loans to the landless – and which has a default rate on those loans of only

49

about 3 per cent – sees loans for the purchase of low-cost vehicles as one of its priority areas. In the decade following its inception in 1976 it funded the purchase of 15,212 vehicles, including over 10,000 rickshaws, 1,800 animal carts and 750 bicycles.[42] The Grameen Bank provides loans for direct income-generating activities – enabling a rickshaw rider to buy his own vehicle, for example – making relatively quick repayment possible. In areas of lesser commercial economic activity, where IMTs would have few directly income-generating applications, the repayment of credit by poor households will prove more difficult. There are, however, alternative ways in which IMTs may be made available in such areas.

The establishment of co-operatives is one way in which individuals can pool their resources to enhance their collective purchasing power. It can be argued, however, that the experience of co-operatives in the developing world is, taken as a whole, less than encouraging. It is also important to note Lele's warning that: 'where traditional power and authority are unequally distributed, cooperatives become an instrument in the hands of the few relatively large farmers and provide little to subsistence farmers.'[43]

Maintenance may also be a problem with co-operatively-owned IMT unless arrangements and responsibility for such work are clearly established. A recent study of ox-cart production and use in Tanzania's Mbeya Region found that all of the eight village-owned carts identified had fallen into disuse within one year of purchase.[44] An alternative approach may be to encourage ownership of IMT by small, self-selected and sustainable groups of villagers.

Another possible way of making IMTs available to those who are neither able to pay for them nor to use them to generate sufficient extra income to repay loans quickly is to offer subsidized credit for their purchase. The government of Burkina Faso assists farmers in poorer parts of the country by offering credit for agricultural equipment, including vehicles, on very soft terms – a five-year repayment period at a very low interest rate. Several other examples of the subsidized distribution of IMTs can be cited. An IDA-supported project in Uganda recently imported 16,000 bicycles which were sold at below commercial market prices – the project was able to do this by importing the bicycles duty-free. The government of the Netherlands made available 35,000 bicycles at subsidized prices as incentive goods to stimulate an increase in agricultural output in three regions of Tanzania. However, such an approach does have implications for the sustainability of the commercial bicycle distribution system, which is also the mechanism for supply of spare parts for maintenance of the bicycles.

Another way in which IMT can be made available to poor people is as partial payment-in-kind for productive work. A World Bank-funded transport project in northern Ghana provides cycle trailers as payment to those providing labour on an allied project to upgrade the local path, track and road network. This intervention addresses several rural transport constraints simultaneously (see Box 2).

Import policy
The import policies pursued by developing country governments can influence the availability of IMTs. Where important types of IMT cannot be made in the country, the only option is to import them. This is most obviously the case with bicycles. In many cases, particularly in African countries, the small size of the internal market makes full local production of cycles economically unviable. There are also certain critical IMT components, such as bearings and tyres, which it is more rational to import into many developing countries than to manufacture locally.

The setting of import tariff rates is a complex issue conditioned, among other factors, by the need to generate national revenue. It is reasonable to argue, however, that the tariff rate set on vehicles and components ought to reflect the value of their contribution to economic and social development. In countries where underdeveloped rural transport facilities act as a constraint on output, the setting of low tariff rates against appropriate vehicles (and necessary components) would be one means of stimulating the agricultural sector – there are examples of countries where import of agricultural equipment is duty-free, but a relatively high tariff is placed on bicycles.

In countries where use of foreign exchange is controlled, the allocation of sufficient resources for import of IMT and components may be an appropriate complementary measure. It is also important to ensure that the distribution of imported IMT is competitive. In Malawi in the 1980s the price of imported bicycles rose very rapidly. The implementation by government of measures to reduce duties, make foreign exchange more easily available, and address the monopoly control over distribution, has resulted in bicycle prices falling to one-third of their peak value in cash terms.

The limitations of intermediate means of transport
While IMTs clearly have a significant role to play in addressing the transport problems faced by rural communities, the limita-

52

tions on the impact which they can have must be recognized. There are theoretical and empirical grounds for questioning the extent to which IMTs will be used for non-agricultural purposes. Studies in a number of countries have found that, even where IMTs exist in some numbers, they are used primarily for agricultural and marketing purposes, and that use for domestic/ subsistence transport purposes is limited. In the case of Aurora, for example, while various IMTs are used by over 75 per cent of households to transport their harvested crops, they are used by only 25 per cent for the collection of firewood and just 7 per cent for the transport of water.

There are rational reasons why priority is given to the use of IMT for agricultural and marketing tasks. First, there may be physical constraints on the suitability of IMT for some domestic transport tasks. For example, if water is collected from a stream at the bottom of a hill, or from a spring, the water source may not be physically accessible by IMT. Similarly, sources of firewood will sometimes only be accessible on foot. For a household which owns oxen and a sledge, it may not be considered worth the effort of harnessing the oxen to the sledge simply to collect water. Second, it should be remembered that, in many situations most poorer households gain access to an IMT by way of hire rather than ownership. They will be reluctant to spend scarce cash, either to hire or buy an IMT, simply to reduce the burden of domestic and subsistence transport tasks. Rather they will be prepared to spend money on transport when the household is particularly busy on a priority activity – most importantly at harvest time – and on activities which will generate a financial return, such as the use of fertilizer and the marketing of crops.

A further limitation to the impact of IMTs, at least in sub-Saharan Africa, relates to the gender division of labour. While African women have primary responsibility for the transport of goods for domestic use, such as firewood and water, they generally enjoy poor access to IMTs. This is due to their generally poor access to cash and to credit facilities; their limited influence over household investment decisions; the fact that IMTs are often regarded as a prestigious possession and are therefore controlled by men; and the existence in many places of strong taboos against the use of IMTs by women. These taboos often apply to the riding of bicycles and the driving of animal carts.

53

The introduction of IMTs has, in a number of documented cases, led to men and boys taking over responsibility for some transport tasks for which women had previously been responsible. In some situations this has occurred because a transport task such as collection of firewood has become a particularly serious problem. Often, however, it has happened only where the activity is commercialized – the transport of water and wood for sale, for example, and the result has sometimes been that women have lost an important source of income. A study into the impact of an oxenization project on women in Tanga, Tanzania, found that, while previously men and women had both derived an income from the transportation and sale of water, wood and crops, young men were the primary beneficiaries of the improved mobility resulting from the project's activities, and were increasingly taking sole responsibility for these functions.[45]

It is on the basis of such cases that Doran has claimed that the introduction of improved forms of transport 'will not necessarily improve womens' welfare even if it reduces their transport burden'. She notes the importance of being aware of the 'different bargaining strengths between household members' in the decision to purchase an IMT and warns of the danger of women losing control over sources of income which they had previously enjoyed.[22]

There is some scope for addressing this issue. The most promising route is actively to direct at rural women the credit facilities which they need for the purchase of IMTs, and to seek to eliminate the taboos against their using the vehicles. An example of such an approach is provided by the World Bank project in Ghana referred to above. Besides targeting credit specifically at women, the provision of cycle trailers is being linked to an educational input from a local community development group aimed at breaking down cultural barriers to the use of bicycles by women.

Development of the local transport infrastructure

The development of rural transport infrastructure will have a central role in a comprehensive strategy to enhance rural mobility. However, it becomes crucially important to ensure that the specification of the infrastructure to be developed, as well as its location, its method of construction, its maintenance and its cost are all appropriate to the transport functions that it will serve and to the means of transport that are likely to use it. A recent World Bank study in sub-Saharan Africa found that: 'Rural transport infrastructure . . . is highly deficient in many countries'.[46] This is true, but it does not imply that a major programme to construct or rehabilitate fully engineered surfaced roads is the sole, appropriate or feasible solution. Indeed, as the same study suggested, the development of 'rural roads and improved tracks navigable (by) animal-drawn vehicles is crucial'.

As part of a comprehensive strategy to enhance rural mobility there are three key aspects to the development and sustainability of appropriate rural transport infrastructure:

o path and track networks;
o low-cost road construction;
o labour-based construction and maintenance methods.

Path and track networks
In most rural areas of developing countries there is an extensive network of footpaths and tracks. These routes link houses to key places in the community – village centre, sources of water and firewood, agricultural land, etc. – and link the community to key places outside – adjacent villages, the roadside and local centres. In general these paths and tracks have not been constructed in the sense that a road is constructed. Rather, they have evolved through continuing use of particular travel routes, perhaps complemented by local efforts to deal with particular trouble spots, for example, the construction of simple means for crossing rivers and streams. The community-level studies emphasize the importance of this track and path network as part of the local transport system. Much of the travel and transport by rural people, within the community and to local places outside, takes place on this path and track network remote from the road. Often, people must first travel along a footpath or track to reach the roadside before undertaking a journey by motor vehicle. Where the condition of a footpath or track makes travel difficult, slow or dangerous, improving its condition would enhance mobility and could be expected to have a significant impact.

There are four circumstances where attention to the condition of footpaths and tracks is likely to be justified:

○ particularly in the wet season, rivers and streams can cause a barrier to travel because of the absence of a suitable crossing, or can be dangerous because the crossing is inadequate. As a consequence people travelling on foot often have to make long detours to find a suitable place to cross, or to risk injury or even death by following the most direct route. There are examples where the poor condition, or absence, of river crossings prevents children from attending school, women from using grinding mills and families from reaching health facilities;

○ many footpaths, particularly over steep terrain or in poor soil conditions, become difficult to traverse in the wet season, causing travel delays. Travel on such routes is more difficult when people are carrying loads;

○ the poor condition of paths and tracks can be a cause of serious accidents. A study in Bangladesh reported that some 50 per cent of broken necks are sustained as a result of falls while carrying loads on the head;[31]

○ paths and tracks which are suitable for travel on foot may need upgrading to facilitate the use of non-motorized IMT.

Some investigations have been carried out to assess the constraints imposed by path and track condition. An ILO study in Makete District showed that the poor condition of the path network was a significant constraint on the mobility and load-carrying capacity of rural communities.[47] A specific problem was the transport of water in the wet season. It was common for women, carrying pails of water on their heads, to slip and fall on the steep paths. Another study, undertaken as part of the Kosi Hill Area Rural Development Programme in Nepal, identified the poor condition of the local infrastructure as a major problem.

There is a range of simple, technical measures which can be implemented to improve track and path condition. These include construction of low-cost timber water crossings; drainage techniques – including very simple structures made from local materials – to prevent paths from becoming slippery; cutting of steps and provision of handrails on steep sections; and simple methods of improving path surface condition.

In certain circumstances, most typically in hilly or mountainous areas, governments and donor agencies have invested in footpath improvements as part of rural infrastructure development programmes. This has happened, for example, in mountainous areas of Nepal and the Philippines. There, the interventions have included construction of suspension footbridges and of cableways, and the paving of important footpaths with stone.

More commonly, constraints on availability of funds and the priority attached to road improvements mean that governments will lack the resources to invest significantly in footpath improvements. In such circumstances, a self-help approach must be adopted. This approach has achieved some success in Makete District in Tanzania, where footpath conditions have been upgraded by the self-help efforts of villagers using local materials, supported by technical advice and assistance with the supply of non-local materials from the local government authority. This approach has the advantages that the skills required for continuing path improvements, and for maintenance, are instilled in the local community. Issues associated with community responsibility for the development of local resources and facilities will be discussed in more detail later in this chapter.

Low-cost road construction
The whole issue of the financing and implementation of road construction and maintenance in developing countries is the subject of considerable attention at present, and the full debate extends beyond the scope of this paper. It is clear, however, that the cost of road construction and maintenance in relation to the resources available is central to this debate. It is therefore important to identify measures to minimize the cost of provision of rural transport infrastructure.

In the context of a comprehensive strategy to enhance rural mobility, a key issue is therefore to provide at minimum cost the necessary level of road access to meet specific transport needs. This implies the need to consider alternatives to the construction of fully-engineered, surfaced, all-weather roads. One strategy is to concentrate limited resources on low-cost measures such as spot improvements in critical sections, surface and side drainage, and essential drainage structures. Such measures can often be sufficient to rehabilitate a deteriorated road, or upgrade an existing track, to a condition that allows essential transport services to serve villages at critical times of the year. The World

Bank project in northern Ghana discussed above is helping local communities to build 'single blade' roads, providing a basic level of access at 8 per cent of the cost per kilometre of conventional feeder roads.[36] Such roads facilitate use of IMTs and can also carry low volumes of motorized traffic.

An alternative strategy is to encourage self-help inputs to rural road improvement and maintenance. While this strategy has some potential it will meet with resistance in some areas, and will often involve considerable community development work to persuade people to participate. Also, self-help road improvement and maintenance should be limited to feeder roads that provide direct access to the participating communities, and must be voluntary rather than enforced. A degree of technical support and supervision will be necessary to ensure that acceptable standards are achieved.

The cost of a road should be assessed over its lifetime, rather than simply on the basis of the initial investment. This emphasizes the fundamental importance of rural road maintenance, both to sustain the level of road access provided (and hence the benefit generated) by the initial investment, and to avoid the need for additional substantial investment after a few years to rehabilitate a road which has deteriorated through neglect. The financing, implementation and management of rural road maintenance is now receiving much greater attention through government and development agency policy initiatives and investment programmes.

Labour-based construction and maintenance methods
There is very substantial scope for the use of labour-based methods for the construction and maintenance of rural roads, and for the improvement of paths and tracks. Efficient labour-based methods do not attempt to execute *all* construction activities using only manual labour. Rather the aim is to employ labour to the maximum extent feasible, but to complement this with appropriate equipment for activities which cannot be executed effectively solely by labour – for example, tractors and trailers may be used to haul materials, and pedestrian rollers to compact earth fill. Labour-based methods are now thoroughly proven to be technically effective for the construction of rural roads and of small structures, and for routine maintenance.

It has also been demonstrated that labour-based methods of road construction are rather cheaper than those which depend on the use of lots of heavy equipment. Under suitable conditions they can yield a saving of about 15 per cent of total costs along with a 40 per cent saving in foreign exchange, for the construction of roads of comparable standard.[48] Thus labour-based methods are both technically effective and cost-efficient. They also create employment and income-earning opportunities in rural areas, eliminate the problems associated with maintenance of complex equipment, and instil skills which can subsequently be applied to road maintenance. Thus, particularly in view of the widespread underemployment and lack of other income-generating activities in many rural areas (particularly during the agricultural slack seasons), the use of labour-based methods simultaneously addresses a number of different problems.

Kenya provides a good example of the potential for labour-based methods. Nearly 10,000km of rural access and minor roads have been rehabilitated, and are now being maintained, by such labour.[49] It has been estimated that the use of purely labour-based methods of maintenance could be applicable to a total of 24,000km (39 per cent) of Kenya's gazetted road network.[50]

The successful and widespread use of labour-based methods involves attention to all aspects of the construction and maintenance process: design, planning, organization, procurement, supervision and management. The development of the national capacity to undertake such work on a large scale can be a long process requiring considerable technical assistance and training support. Successful initiatives supported by the ILO in this field have typically needed to be sustained over periods of up to 10 years in order to achieve a substantial impact. This clearly requires a long-term commitment from both governments and development agencies.

A recent initiative is to encourage the participation of national contractors in the application of labour-based construction and maintenance methods. An ILO report argues that, although in technical terms few difficulties are encountered, 'there is no real future for the use of labour-based techniques if they are not taken over by the private sector.'[48] The ILO has found that local contractors participating in projects which it has supported – and

59

especially the smaller operators who are likely to be particularly active in the labour-based construction market – have needed considerable support. This has included management training, especially in terms of financial planning. Other problems which small-scale contractors tend to face relate to poor access to credit and shortages of working capital as a result of delays in payment for work completed. These problems can be overcome only by concerted government action.

Transport services

The third major element (of those noted on page 40) in enhancing the mobility of rural people is the development of rural transport services. To date governments and development agencies have tended to give limited attention to this, largely restricting themselves to involvement in road infrastructure investments. Given that levels of ownership of motor vehicles in rural areas are generally very low, the mechanism by which the mobility of rural people and their goods will increase as a result of road improvements is through the operation of transport services. The emphasis on investment in road infrastructure suggests an implicit assumption that private and public sector operators of transport services will respond efficiently to the opportunities opened up. One report went as far as complaining that: 'The planners' assumption must be that vehicles and transport services will materialise as if by magic.'[6]

Yet, in many parts of the developing world, such vehicles and transport services have largely failed to materialize. Data cited in Chapter 3 on traffic counts in various countries confirm that the existence of rural roads able to carry motorized traffic is in many cases insufficient to guarantee high levels of such traffic. In such cases, the availability of local-level, affordable transport services would serve to enhance the mobility of rural people to reach markets for their crops, sources of farm inputs and health and educational facilities.

As a consequence of the relative neglect of rural transport services as an area of policy intervention, there are few examples of positive measures which have been introduced. There is, none the less, considerable potential for interventions to promote increased use of rural roads by motor vehicles. One strategy is to encourage private transport operators to increase their activities in the rural areas by reducing the constraints imposed by regulations which often control the transport service market. A World Bank study of six countries in Africa and Asia[4] identified high levels of government control over transport services as a central factor in explaining the generally low level of motor-vehicle traffic on rural roads. It found a wide range of restrictions, including high barriers to entry and the exclusion of private operators from certain markets; control over routes; restrictions on fares (often with little or no account taken of the higher costs and lower returns involved in operating on rural roads); restrictions on the combined transport of passengers and freight; and poor access for private operators to imported spare parts.

There can be no disputing the need for government to exercise some control over the transport service market, particularly in relation to the safety of the service. Unfortunately, unnecessary restrictions of the type described above are common in many countries and there is considerable scope for relaxing controls in a way that compromises neither the safety nor the welfare of the users of the service. Of particular importance is that transport operators be allowed to set their fares at levels which reflect the real costs of operating their services on rural roads. Such a policy initiative would contribute to addressing a situation that exists in many countries, namely that transport services are concentrated on principal, long-distance routes where operating costs are lowest and the highest profits can be made.

There are many situations, however, where additional incentives may be necessary to encourage private operators to provide local-level 'feeder' transport services on rural roads, rather than focusing on main routes. Such incentives could take the form of subsidies agreed with transport operators to encourage them to begin services in certain areas. There are of course risks in subsidizing transport operations and such subsidies should be subject to regular review with a view to reducing or, ideally, phasing them out altogether as operators gain experience of the routes and are able to tailor their services to the needs of the areas.

An innovative pilot project has been designed to address the notable lack of local-level transport services in rural areas of Malawi. The approach adopted is to offer credit, in the form of a leasing arrangement, for purchase of medium-sized passenger- and goods-carrying vehicles, conditional upon them being operated within a 40–50km radius of local rural centres. This financing will be accompanied by training in vehicle operation and maintenance. The pilot project aims to confirm the feasibility of such services and to demonstrate how they can be financed and operated effectively.

Credit can also be provided to enable a village, co-operative or community development organization to purchase their own vehicle. Experience available of this approach suggests that financing support should be linked to training in the management, operation and maintenance of a truck or bus service, in order to ensure financial viability. A key issue in management is to guarantee that maintenance over the lifetime of the vehicle is fully costed, and that a proportion of revenue is set aside to cover subsequent maintenance costs.

Another approach to increasing the volume of motorized traffic in the rural areas is the provision of transport services by central or local government. There are examples of bus services operated by local government councils and cargo services provided by marketing boards or co-operative organizations. It is important to recognize that such services have often proved unsustainable, in part at least due to poor financial management. But there are also examples of success. A national milk co-operative in India, for instance, collects nearly three million litres of milk daily, produced by two million farmers, from designated collection points by the roadside.[8] The District Development Funds in Zimbabwe own trucks which they hire out to communities for the transport of their harvest to the nearest crop purchasing points. The possibility of refining and replicating such successful schemes, especially in areas of high agricultural output, is worth exploring.

More generally, it can be argued that the preparation and appraisal of rural road investment schemes should be accompanied by an assessment of the likelihood that transport services will develop to operate on the road and that, if necessary, complementary measures should be designed to stimulate the operation of such services. Two recent examples of the incorporation of such complementary measures in the design of investments that include rural road improvements, are the provision of a foreign-currency credit for the import of trucks, and the inclusion of a project component to develop local vehicle maintenance and repair capability.

It is not only conventional motor vehicles that can provide rural transport services. In some Asian countries, low-cost, *motorized* means of transport are used to provide such services. The vehicles used include three-wheeled devices powered by single-cylinder diesel engines, and motor cycles and trailers. Perhaps the best example is in the Philippines where motor cycles and side-cars, known as motor tricycles, provide extensive rural transport services. Their services link up the many villages to main roads where more conventional transport services operate. They complement by feeding into and extending the impact of transport services provided by buses, minibuses and trucks. The low capital and running costs of these vehicles allow them to operate profitable, local-level services on routes where there is insufficient demand to justify the operation of larger vehicles.

There is also a need to explore the potential for the development of local-level transport services using non-motorized IMT. Several examples of such schemes are already in place: the Milk Vita Company in Bangladesh uses rickshaw vans (a pedal tricycle adapted to carry cargo loads) to collect milk from its farmers; marketing facilities provided by some farmers' co-operatives to their members in Gujarat State in India include bullock carts for the transport of crops.[33] Such non-motorized transport services will tend be most in demand and most effective where there is a large volume of goods needing to be moved over relatively short distances and where their availability will permit either a significant cost saving or a large increase in marketed output. It should also be noted that, in riverine areas, extensive rural transport services can be provided by small boats powered by sail, oars or small diesel engines. In Bangladesh, boats constitute an important element of the rural transport system. There appears to be some scope for community groups or co-operatives to become involved in the management of IMT services.

Transport services can address the external transport problems faced by rural people which were identified by the community-level studies. The development of local-level transport services represents a fresh area for policy initiatives, with considerable potential, which needs to be explored with some urgency by policymakers and planners.

Reducing the need for rural travel and transport

A holistic approach to addressing the problems associated with rural transport involves a move beyond an exclusive focus on measures to improve mobility by making travel faster, cheaper or less burdensome. It also incorporates the option of 'non-transport' policy measures and interventions to increase accessibility by reducing or obviating the need for travel by rural people. 'Non-transport' interventions to improve accessibility for rural communities fall into two broad categories:

○ the location of facilities;

○ storage and credit provision.

Location of facilities
Key determinants of patterns of travel for a particular purpose are the distance to the facility involved, and the means of transport used. These determine the time and effort involved per trip, and also influence (to a greater or lesser extent for different trip purposes) the frequency of trips. Hence they determine the total time and effort involved in fulfilling the transport task. Measures to improve mobility through use of IMTs, improvement of infrastructure and development of transport services, will increase accessibility by reducing the time and/or effort involved per trip, and so can also be expected to stimulate some increased use of the facility. Trip time and effort can also be reduced, and accessibility increased, by reducing the distance that people have to travel to reach facilities. Thus the location of facilities (such as water and firewood sources; agricultural input supply centres and crop marketing facilities; grinding mills; clinics and schools) in relation to the rural communities that use them is a key determinant of the scale and nature of the transport burden. There is scope to reduce this burden, and increase the efficiency of transport, by locating such facilities closer to rural communities.

A degree of caution is necessary in making generalized statements about which facilities should receive priority in terms of locating them closer to communities, since the circumstances of different areas in terms of accessibility will differ, and local resource planning should vary accordingly. There is, none the less, considerable evidence from the community-level studies – as

64

well as from complementary research cited earlier – to suggest that water and firewood collection figure prominently in the transport workloads of many rural households. In the community-level studies, over half of all trips and about a quarter of all time spent by households on transport tasks was devoted to the collection of water. Firewood collection also constituted a substantial drain on the households' time and energy budgets in each of the study areas. Further, there is evidence that the burden of firewood collection is increasing in many areas – deforestation, exacerbated by increasing population pressure, means that people are forever having to travel farther to reach wood sources.

There are limitations on the impact which measures to increase mobility can have on improving access to water supplies. These include the limited availability of IMTs (particularly to women) and their technical unsuitability for collection of water from many natural sources. Using IMTs can reduce the burden of firewood collection, but there is a significant risk that this will exacerbate the problem of deforestation by encouraging increased consumption. This suggests that some emphasis should therefore be given to addressing the transport problems of water and firewood collection by 'non-transport' interventions. In the case of water, the most effective policy is to provide improved water supplies closer to rural communities. In the case of firewood collection the policy options include the establishment of community wood-lots and the dissemination of fuel-efficient cooking stoves (to reduce demand for firewood). Rural electrification is likely to have less impact since the main use of electricity is for lighting. Using electricity for cooking entails investment in a suitable stove, and relatively high running costs. In mountainous regions, however, small-scale micro-hydro technologies may have potential with the recent development of low-cost storage cookers.

Such measures can be expected to have a significant impact in reducing the transport burden of these essential domestic tasks, and hence in freeing household labour resources for more beneficial activities. The case of Tanzania illustrates this in respect of water supply. In Makete the average walking time to a source of water is 23 minutes and the typical household spends about 645 hours per annum on transporting water. The national target is that all rural households should be within 400 metres of a source of potable water. This implies a walking time of about six minutes and, at a constant rate of consumption, would reduce the time spent per annum to about 170 hours, a saving of 475 hours per annum or nearly 10 hours every week. Clearly, such policies to improve the supply of water and fuel are also likely to have wider benefits, including improved health resulting from access to clean water, and a reduction in the rate of deforestation.

The response to the location of a facility closer to a community may be more complex than simply a proportionate reduction in the transport burden for that task. Some research has found that improved access to water and firewood for communities which had previously been relatively distant from them may not significantly reduce the total workload involved in their collection since consumption levels rise quite sharply.[51] None the less, if households continue to devote similar total amounts of time to water and firewood collection it is presumably because they place high priority on the improved welfare benefits which accrue from increased consumption in terms of better health and greater capacity for cleaning and cooking. The fundamental point is that reducing the distance to a facility increases the efficiency of transport. That is it increases the return to the investment of a given amount of transport time and effort. The benefits of this increased efficiency may be manifested as a reduction in the transport burden, increased utilization of the facility, or a combination of the two.

A similar argument applies to the provision of rural health centres, grinding mills, input supply centres and crop marketing facilities for communities which were previously remote from them. The likely result is that people will make *greater* use of those facilities. This may imply increased time spent on travel for this purpose, but with the attendant benefits of better health care, reduction in time spent on pounding food, or increased income from agriculture.

It must be emphasized that there are limitations on the extent to which access to health-care, food-processing and agricultural facilities can be improved by dispersing their locations. For example a health-care facility must have a sufficiently large catchment population to justify the investment in the building and the employment of health personnel. A grinding mill will only be financially viable if the demand for its services exceeds a certain break-even point. Where fixed facilities are not viable,

66

however, there remains potential for delivery of mobile services to communities, to reduce the distance that they need to travel. The possibilities include mobile health clinics, delivery of farm inputs to communities, and crop purchasing and collection services.

Governments and development agencies have only limited resources and capacity to install improved water supplies, to develop wood-lots, and to construct and operate farm input supply centres, crop-marketing facilities, clinics and schools. The provision of services and facilities at the local level in developing countries, however, is not the sole preserve of the state. In fact, it is increasingly recognized that initiatives of this type can successfully be planned, implemented and managed by NGOs, self-help and community groups. A recent World Bank report on these issues concluded: 'National and even regional governments cannot effectively manage local natural resources. Programmes and projects must become more concerned with the people using the natural resources and less preoccupied with the commodities around which projects have traditionally been organised. Natural resource projects that do not actively incorporate the local users will fail.'[34]

It is increasingly the practice, in rural water-supply programmes, to focus on small-scale local-level schemes; community participation in planning and implementation; and community responsibility for management and operation, including the financing of maintenance. Similarly in the health-care sector there is increasing emphasis on developing community-financed village health-worker services. There are examples of successful community-based, forestry-management programmes, perhaps the most famous of which is Kenya's Green Belt Movement which has sponsored a significant degree of afforestation. In the Gambia, the National Women's Bureau and the Forestry Department have promoted the establishment of wood-lots managed by village women's groups which today produce large quantities of fuelwood. Villagers in the Nepalese highlands have been running their own forestry-management schemes since the 1960s.

Having acknowledged the central role of rural communities in the design, implementation and management of local initiatives, it is important not to overlook the key role of central and local government in this process. Their functions can be broadly described as follows:

o active support to the formation and strengthening of local community groups;

o decentralization of some operations of specialist technical government departments such as forestry, water and health to enable them to provide effective support to communities and groups – in the form of training and skill development, extension, and supervisory and back-up services to address technical and managerial problems;

o improving the access of local community groups to necessary tools and equipment and inputs such as seedlings and building materials;

o the provision of budgets to regional and district authorities for the purchase of equipment and materials, and the provision of other inputs to support community initiatives;

o a reorientation of the training/education strategy to produce technicians and other rural development staff with the appropriate skills to work alongside, and support, rural communities.

The community-oriented approach has a number of strengths. It gives communities the opportunity to exercise control over the supply of, and develop a sense of ownership about, those resources to which they need access. By acquiring the skills necessary to establish and manage their own facilities, local communities can significantly reduce their level of dependence on governments whose resources are, in many cases, becoming increasingly stretched. Recent research in Zambia found a strong positive correlation between high levels of community participation in rural water programmes and the long-term maintenance of the well equipment.[52]

Community management of, and responsibility for, resources is likely to lead to more careful and less wasteful usage. For example, the introduction of IMT to provide easier access to firewood is likely to result in increased consumption, with the attendant danger of an accelerated depletion of the forest resource. The introduction of wood-lots, on the other hand, represents at least a partial replenishment of what is consumed. .

The location of facilities closer to the people can have a significant impact on many of the transport problems identified in the community-level surveys. The effective implementation of this approach, however, requires considerable political will to devolve responsibility to local communities and, within the government structure, to decentralize functions and decision-making authority, particularly in relation to planning, implementation and financial control.

Storage and credit provision

The provision of storage facilities is a 'non-transport' intervention which, in certain circumstances, can address the transport problem related to crop marketing. In some parts of the Third World, the storage facilities to be found at village level are insufficient for the needs of all farmers in the community. This leaves farmers with little choice but to sell much of their produce at low prices at harvest-time when there is a glut of crops on the market, and to buy food later in the year, in the hungry months before the next harvest, at a considerably higher price. The problem is exacerbated as a result of the debts incurred by many households – often to traders or to suppliers of farm inputs – which puts further pressure on them to sell much of their crop at harvest-time.

The result is that even in 'subsistence' or 'food-deficit' areas, farmers often spend significant amounts of time and energy transporting crops to and from the market. (It will be recalled that the distances to be travelled to market in the transport study areas ranged from two hours in Aurora to four hours in Makete.) A 1985 study in Bangladesh found that: 'in one of the study areas, between 30 and 40 per cent of the rice paddy is sold within two weeks of harvest either to repay debts (to traders) or because of lack of storage.'[16]

Efforts to reduce the need for farmers to sell crops immediately after the harvest would have the dual effect of enabling them to earn more from their produce and reducing the scale of the crop-marketing transport burden. This is likely to require a two-track approach involving the provision of both storage facilities and credit. The Bangladeshi NGO, BRAC, has recently introduced such a programme, with initially favourable results, in several of the areas where it works. Farmers are paid at the going price when they deposit their crops in the BRAC silos. The farmers sell their produce on the open market when they choose, repaying to BRAC the original amount received and keeping the balance.

69

There are grounds for believing that NGOs may be more suited to administering schemes of this sort than government. To date they have proved more successful at developing small-scale credit and other assistance programmes aimed at the rural poor, greater flexibility being their key strength. Governments may have an important role in supporting – and perhaps initially financing – the efforts of NGOs to learn from the experience of successful initiatives of this sort elsewhere and to develop programmes appropriate to their own countries.

The complementarity of interventions to address rural transport problems

This chapter has presented a range of options for addressing rural transport problems in developing countries. These include measures to enhance rural mobility through increased use of IMT, improvement of rural transport infrastructure, and development of local transport services; and measures to reduce the need for travel and transport by locating facilities closer to communities that will use them, and provision of storage facilities and associated credit.

It is important first to emphasize that the different measures to enhance mobility are complementary. In many situations their impact will be enhanced by implementing two, or all three, of the measures simultaneously. Some examples of this have already been given. It is desirable to consider the need for inputs to promote the operation of transport services as a complement to investment in the rural road network. The use of IMT may be facilitated by upgrading footpaths and tracks.

The Ghana project referred to earlier is an example of using a labour-based road construction programme to promote the use of IMTs by offering these in partial payment for work on the roads. The most efficient way of hauling construction materials over short distances on labour-based rural road projects is often to use IMTs such as wheelbarrows and animal-drawn carts. When IMTs are used in such projects, two complementary rural transport constraints can be tackled in tandem: the use of IMTs can be demonstrated and popularized at the same time as improving the standard of the transport infrastructure.

More generally there is a case to be argued for maximizing the

70

impact of rural road investments, and the use of the roads that are improved, not just by developing transport services, but also by measures which will feed more traffic from the 'off-road' system into the road network, that is, by upgrading paths and tracks and promoting IMT.

It was stated earlier that enhancing mobility and reducing the need for travel and transport constitute the two complementary elements of a comprehensive strategy to tackle the transport burden shouldered by rural communities. It must be stressed that these two elements are complementary and should certainly not be regarded as competing, alternative strategies. There are several practical respects in which the two approaches are complementary. The provision and effective operation of facilities located close to rural communities, sometimes off the road network, will require the availability of appropriate transport. For example:

○ the involvement of communities in implementation of improved water-supply projects will require that they have access to IMT for short-distance hauling of materials. Also, the village 'mechanics' responsible for maintenance of the system will need transport to obtain spare parts;

○ village health workers need to be mobile in order to travel around the community, and to reach a centre outside the village to obtain supplies and medical support. Transport is needed to deliver supplies to rural health centres or clinics, and for medical personnel to travel there;

○ the operation of a grinding mill is dependent on transport to deliver fuel, and for supply of spare parts;

○ the construction of local-level facilities involves the transport of materials and technical personnel to the site.

The operation of the Forestry Department in Andra Pradesh provides an example of the complementarity of local facilities and IMT. The department has established local nurseries (for the supply of seedlings) which are serviced by cycle trailers. Agricultural production and marketing is another field in which it is desirable that policies of provision of facilities and of transport should be implemented in tandem. The provision of farm input supply, storage and purchasing facilities can stimulate increased

71

production. However, without the capacity to transport greater volumes of inputs to the land and increased harvests from it, farmers will not be able to respond fully to the opportunity presented. This was recognized by planners in Zimbabwe who, as part of a package of assistance, including better marketing facilities, offered credit to farmers to enable them to purchase animal carts. The increased density of crop purchasing points together with the improved availability of these carts have stimulated substantial increases in smallholder agricultural output. Neither intervention on its own would have achieved comparable results.

The findings from the community-level studies demonstrate the importance of transport to rural people in meeting many of their subsistence, economic and social needs. They also indicate that rural people face a range of different transport problems. The analysis of policies to address these problems shows that there a range of measures which can be applied. Different measures will address different transport needs, but are likely to be most effective if a range of complementary measures are applied simultaneously. This argues the case for an integrated, area-based approach to the planning of interventions to address rural transport problems. This approach has two key advantages:

○ it takes the transport needs of rural communities as its starting point, and recognizes that a number of factors which influence the nature and extent of transport problems are location-specific, for example, population density, settlement patterns, terrain, agricultural characteristics, level of development, etc.;

○ it allows an integrated package of complementary measures to be defined which respond in the most effective manner to the range and balance of transport problems in a particular area. In so doing it facilitates the efficient allocation of scarce resources between different measures.

It is precisely this approach that has been adopted by the ILO in the Philippines to follow up the community-level studies carried out there. A Rural Transport Unit (RTU) has been established which has developed a methodology for identifying, and defining the most effective package of measures to respond to, the priority rural transport problems in a particular area. With training and advisory support from the RTU, this methodology is now being applied by local government planning offices in different parts of the country. The development and application of this methodology has been most timely since it has taken place in parallel with a major government initiative to decentralize responsibility for development planning and implementation. Local government units in the Philippines now have substantial responsibility for planning of development activities and for allocation of funds to different activities.

In the context of decentralization in the Philippines, this integrated, local-level, area-based approach to planning of rural transport improvements has proved to have another advantage. Prior to decentralization, there was a lack of planning capacity at local level. In particular there was a lack of capacity to prioritize development investments, and allocate scarce resources, in a rational manner rather than defining 'shopping-lists' of desirable activities that bear little relationship to available resources. Because transport is a factor in so many different aspects of rural development, the application of the methodology has proved to be an effective entry-point to local-level rural development planning. It provides local-level planners with appropriate, practical tools to collect planning data, and to analyse this data (including community participation in the process) in order to derive rational planning decisions on many aspects of rural development.

5

Transport and rural development

THE TIME HAS COME for the issue of transport to assume a more prominent position in rural development planning. A growing body of literature identifies tight labour constraints at certain peak periods of the farming calendar in parts of the developing world. At the same time the community-level studies, complemented by a substantial volume of related research, point to transport as being a major drain on the time and energy budgets of rural households.

There are indications that, in the absence of concerted action, the rural transport burden is likely to increase in scale. The progressive depletion of resources, particularly fuelwood, will exacerbate the transport problems associated with their use. Meanwhile, the need for increased production of both foodstuffs for growing domestic populations and cash crops for export to repay debts and earn foreign exchange can only add to the transport load – in terms of the volume of goods to be carried by rural people and of the distances to be covered.

The material here has argued that to continue to define rural transport in terms of 'roads and motor vehicles', and to concentrate policies and investments on the development of rural road networks, is not enough. Rather the need is for governments and development agencies to adopt a broader vision, and to complement rural road investment with other measures which address in a more holistic way the totality of the accessibility needs of rural populations.

There is growing evidence, as is demonstrated by the many examples of positive interventions cited in this paper, that both governments and development agencies are becoming persuaded of the wisdom of this course of action. There remains, none the less, much potential for the wider replication of both the location-specific planning techniques proposed here and the policy measures and interventions recommended.

This holistic approach entails the rational planning of interventions, and the allocation of resources, in response to the real accessibility needs of the communities in particular rural areas. The interventions will include a mix of measures to enhance mobility and to provide facilities which will reduce the need for travel and transport. The balance of the mix will depend on the local conditions prevailing in the area. This area-based planning approach can provide an entry point to more comprehensive, rural development planning responsive to local needs.

It is worth remembering in this context that many of the measures proposed in this paper do not involve a major financial outlay. In many cases, in fact, the efficiency and sustainability of the interventions are likely to be enhanced if relatively low-cost, labour-intensive strategies are chosen. This does, however, require a shift in the role of government services away from implementation and towards the provision of advice, support, training, credit, equipment and materials. Services of this nature can generally be most successfully delivered by an effective, well-resourced, decentralized system.

The transport burden faced by rural communities in many parts of the developing world is of substantial proportions. It often acts as a constraint (either actual or potential) on economic activity as well as on the social development of rural communities. Concerted action to reduce the drudgery and waste of time associated with long hours spent walking and carrying loads will make a substantial contribution to increasing agricultural productivity, together with enhancing the welfare of rural dwellers.

References

1. ILO, *Appropriate Transport Facilities for the Rural Sector in Developing Countries*, Geneva 1979.
2. Kaira, K., *Transportation Needs of the Rural Population in Developing Countries*, IFR, 1983.
3. Edmonds, G. and Relf, C., Background and Discussion Paper on International Meeting on Transport and Development, 10–11 October 1985.
4. IBRD, *The Supply and Quality of Rural Transport Services in Developing Countries: A Comparative Review*, Washington 1984.
5. Barwell, I. *et al.*, *Appropriate Transport Facilities for the Rural Sector in Developing Countries*, UNIDO, 1978.
6. Johnston, D.C., 'Rural Transport in South East Asia: Pointers Toward the Twenty-First Century', Paper presented to Commonwealth Geographical Bureau Workshop, Chinese University of Hong Kong, December 1990.
7. Smillie, I., *Mastering The Machine*, IT Publications, London 1991.
8. Owen, W., *Transport and World Development*, Hutchinson, London 1987.
9. IBRD, *Ghana: Policies and Programme for Adjustment*, Washington 1984.
10. Barwell, I. *et al.*, 'Position Paper on Rural Mobility in Developing Countries', IT Transport, 1988.
11. Relf, C. and Dixon-Fyle, K., *Local-Level Transport in Malawi: Report of an Exploratory Mission*, ILO, June 1988.
12. SEATAC, *Study of Transport Investment and Impact on Distribution of Income in Remote Areas*, 1979.
13. Howe, J. and Richards, P., *Rural Roads and Poverty Alleviation*, IT Publications, 1984.
14. Leinbach, T.R., 'Rural Transport and Population Mobility in Indonesia', *The Journal of Developing Areas*, Vol. 17, April 1983.

15. Blaikie, P. *et al.*, *The Effects of Roads in West Central Nepal*, ODA, 1977.

16. Barwell, I. *et al.*, *Rural Transport in Developing Countries*, IT Publications, 1985.

17. Chambers, R. *et al.* (eds.), *Seasonal Dimensions to Rural Poverty*, Pinter, 1981.

18. Carr, M., 'The Long Walk Home', in *Appropriate Technology*, Vol. 10, No. 1, 1983.

19. Curtis, V., *Women and the Transport of Water*, IT Publications, 1986.

20. IBRD, *Village Water Supply*, Washington 1976.

21. ECAFE, Transport and Communications Committee, 1969.

22. Doran, J., 'A Moving Issue for Women: Is Low-Cost Transport an Appropriate Intervention to Alleviate Women's Burdens in Southern Africa?', MA Thesis, University of East Anglia, 1989.

23. Barwell, I. and Leggett, I., *Study on Promotion of Rural Transport in Tanga Region*, Tanzania, GTZ, 1986.

24. Barwell, I. and Malmberg-Calvo, C., 'Makete Integrated Rural Transport Project: The Transport Demands of Rural Households: Findings from a Village Level Travel Survey', ILO, Geneva 1988.

25. Howe, J. and Barwell, I., 'Study of Potential for Intermediate Means of Transport in Ghana', for Ministry of Transport and Communications, 1987.

26. Barwell, I., 'Household Travel Demand in Aurora Province', ILO, 1989.

27. Barwell, I., 'Findings from Preliminary Analysis of Mountain Province Household Survey', ILO, Manila 1990.

28. Donnges, C., 'Findings from Preliminary Analysis of Ifugao Province Household Survey', ILO, Manila 1991.

29. SWECO, *Draft Final Report on National Transport Study*, People's Democratic Republic of Laos, 1990.

30. Riverson, J.D. and Carapetis, S., 'The Potential of Intermediate Means of Transport in Improving Rural Travel and Transport in Sub-Saharan Africa', Paper Presented to Conference on Low-Volume Roads, 19–23 May 1991, North Carolina State University.

31. Asian Development Bank, *Bangladesh Second Rural Infrastructure Development Project*, Feasibility Study, 1991.

32. Marsh, D.K. and Taylor, G.A., *The Movement of Goods and*

People in the Kosi Hills, KHARDEP Report No. 37, Government of Nepal, 1982.

33. Sardesai, K.V., *Rural Transport Equipment for Agricultural Freight in Asia*, UNIDO, Vienna 1989.
34. IBRD, *Agriculture, Population and Environment Nexus in Sub-Saharan Africa*, Washington 1990.
35. Rogers, B., *The Domestication of Women*, Tavistock, London 1980.
36. Ecoforum, Vol. 7, No. 3, London 1988.
37. IBRD, *From Crisis to Sustainable Growth*, Washington 1989.
38. Starkey, P., 'Animal-Drawn Transport in Africa', in *Transport for the Poor*, GATE, Germany 1989.
39. Hughes, K. and Replogle, M., 'Sustainable Transportation: Options for the Poor', in *Transport for the Poor*, GATE, Germany 1989.
40. IT Transport, *Improving Animal-Based Transport in Eastern and Southern Africa*, UK 1992.
41. IT Transport, *The ITDG Kenya Animal-Cart Project*, UK 1989.
42. Grameen Bank, Annual Report 1986, Dhaka, Bangladesh.
43. Lele, U., *The Design of Rural Development: Lessons from Africa*, Johns Hopkins, London 1975.
44. Shetto, R.M. and Kwiligna, E.M., 'Survey of Ox-Cart Use in Mbeya Region', Mbeya Oxenisation Project, Tanzania 1988.
45. Lauer, M., 'The Impact of the Oxenisation Project at Mwanyumba on Women', Tanga, TIRDEP.
46. Riverson, J. *et al.*, *Rural Roads in Sub-Saharan Africa: Lessons from World Bank Experience*, IBRD, Washington 1991.
47. Dixon-Fyle, K. and Frieling, I., *Paths in Rural Transport*, ILO, Geneva 1990.
48. Edmonds, G. and de Veen, J., *Technology Choice for the Construction and Maintenance of Roads in Developing Countries*, ILO, Geneva 1991.
49. Ministry of Public Works, Kenya, 'Rural Access Roads Programme and Minor Roads Programme', Progress Report No. 12, 1992.
50. Ministry of Public Works, Kenya, Minor Roads Transition Programme Transition Project Proposal, 1991.
51. Carr, M. and Sandhu, R., *Women, Technology and Rural*

78

Productivity: An Analysis of the Impact of Time and Energy-Saving Technologies on Women, IT Consultants, 1987.

52. Sutton, S.E. and Sutton, J.S., 'Rural Water Supply: Infrastructure Development', in *Appropriate Development for Basic Needs*, Thomas Telford, London 1991.